*THE CITIZEN'S LIBRARY OF ECONOMICS, POLITICS
AND SOCIOLOGY—NEW SERIES*

Edited by RICHARD T. ELY, Ph.D., LL.D.
Professor of Political Economy in the University of Wisconsin

THE SOCIAL PROBLEM

THE CITIZEN'S LIBRARY OF ECONOMICS POLITICS AND SOCIOLOGY

EDITED BY

RICHARD T. ELY, PH.D., LL.D.

Professor of Political Economy in the University
of Wisconsin

NEW SERIES

THE PROGRESSIVE MOVEMENT. By BENJAMIN P. DEWITT, M.A., LL.B.

THE SOCIAL PROBLEM. By CHARLES A. ELLWOOD, PH.D. New and greatly enlarged edition.

THE WEALTH AND INCOME OF THE PEOPLE OF THE UNITED STATES. By WILLFORD I. KING, PH.D.

THE FOUNDATIONS OF NATIONAL PROSPERITY. By RICHARD T. ELY, PH.D., LL.D.; RALPH H. HESS, PH.D.; CHARLES K. LEITH, PH.D.; THOMAS NIXON CARVER, PH.D., LL.D.

THE WORLD WAR AND LEADERSHIP IN A DEMOCRACY. By RICHARD T. ELY, PH.D., LL.D.

BUDGET MAKING IN A DEMOCRACY. By MAJOR EDWARD A. FITZPATRICK.

THE VISION FOR WHICH WE FOUGHT. By A. M. SIMONS, B.L.

CITY MANAGER IN DAYTON. By CHESTER E. RIGHTOR, B.A.

THE SOCIAL PROBLEM

A RECONSTRUCTIVE ANALYSIS

BY

CHARLES A. ELLWOOD, Ph. D.,

PROFESSOR OF SOCIOLOGY IN THE UNIVERSITY OF MISSOURI,
AUTHOR OF "INTRODUCTION TO SOCIAL PSY-
CHOLOGY," "SOCIOLOGY AND MODERN
SOCIAL PROBLEMS," ETC.

REVISED EDITION

New York
THE MACMILLAN COMPANY
1927

PRINTED IN THE UNITED STATES OF AMERICA BY
THE BERWICK & SMITH CO.

TO THE FAR THINKING MEN AND WOMEN
OF THE TWENTIETH CENTURY, WHO
MUST SOLVE THE SOCIAL PROBLEM

PREFATORY NOTE

THE original purpose of this little book was to furnish an outline of progressive social principles, upon the basis of a brief analysis of the social problem, for use in social reconstruction after the War. Written in Oxford, England, during the first three months of the War, the great prolongation of the destructive struggle and the consequent demand for radical reconstruction of our civilization to prevent the recurrence of such a calamity might seem to call for radical revision of the book. Fortunately, however, the principles outlined were so general that it has been found necessary only to shift their emphasis and elaborate certain points. The principles themselves will be found not less applicable than in 1914.

It has been becoming more evident than ever that the War calls, first and foremost, for a reconstruction of our social philosophy, and that we cannot safely rebuild our civilization upon the inadequate bases of nineteenth-century thought. The book aims to indicate the direction which our social thinking must take if we are to avoid revolution, on the one hand, and reaction, on the other. It aims, in other words, to furnish a scientific basis for progressive, in distinction from revolutionary or reactionary, social reconstruction. Hence it strives to take a constructive attitude toward all essential elements in our civilization.

The full scientific evidence for the sociological principles invoked and the conclusions drawn must, of course, be sought by the critical reader in the author's other books, especially in his *Introduction to Social Psychology*. In these also will be found lists of authorities and references in support of the positions taken.

CHARLES A. ELLWOOD.

University of Missouri,
June, 1919.

CONTENTS

ix

CONTENTS

CHAPTER III

PHYSICAL AND BIOLOGICAL ELEMENTS IN THE SOCIAL PROBLEM

CHAPTER IV

ECONOMIC ELEMENTS IN THE SOCIAL PROBLEM

CONTENTS

CHAPTER V

SPIRITUAL AND IDEAL ELEMENTS IN THE SOCIAL PROBLEM

CHAPTER VI

THE EDUCATIONAL ELEMENT IN THE SOCIAL PROBLEM

CONTENTS

CHAPTER VII

THE SOLUTION OF THE SOCIAL PROBLEM

THE SOCIAL PROBLEM

THE SOCIAL PROBLEM

A RECONSTRUCTIVE ANALYSIS

CHAPTER I

THE PROBLEM STATED [1]

THE Great War has rendered it unnecessary to prove to anyone that something is radically wrong with our civilization; and that radical reconstruction of its spirit and institutions is needed. The foolish sense of security and the shallow optimism which prior to the War led whole classes to ignore or deride the warnings given by careful students of social and political conditions, scarcely longer exist. In their stead has come

[1] Parts of this chapter were presented in a paper before the Sociological Society (London), Nov. 10, 1914, on "The Social Problem and the Present War," which was later (January, 1915) published simultaneously in the *Sociological Review* and the *American Journal of Sociology*.

widespread apprehension and pessimism. The troubles of our civilization, it is felt, may be just beginning rather than ending with the close of the War. Yet if we could think alike; if we could be united and not divided; if we could learn to work together harmoniously at the essential tasks of life, we could not only bear the burdens which the War has brought us, but we could build a much worthier civilization than any dreamed of by the nineteenth century.

Not that there is no ground for apprehension. On the contrary, just at present the atmosphere of the world seems charged with revolution. Not only in Russia, but in all the great civilized nations an apparently increasing number look to a proletarian revolution to straighten out matters. The blindness and selfishness of some in our socially privileged classes, the fanatic radicalism and class hatred of some of the leaders of the non-privileged, moreover, threaten to frustrate all attempts to reëstablish harmony and good will in our divided world.

Yet if the Great War is to be succeeded by

a series of civil and international wars, if relatively permanent peace, social as well as international, is not to intervene to heal the wounds of the world and give opportunity to lighten its burdens, then the outlook is bad indeed for Western civilization. What we face is not merely the dangers of a political and economic revolution brought about by force, but the possibility of one of those long swing-backs in human culture which seem to come about every fifteen hundred years. Careful students of civilization, even prior to the War, have frequently pointed out the disturbing resemblances between our civilization and that of decadent Rome.[2] No extended scientific research is necessary to establish the parallel. The very forces which undermined the civilization of the Ancient World, namely, national imperialism, militarism, commercialism, materialistic standards of life, class conflicts, individualism, agnosticism in religion and ethics, a low

[2] See especially Ferrero, *Ancient Rome and Modern America*, Chapter IV of Part Two.

estimate of marriage and the family, are the things which are just now prominent, if not dominant, in the civilization of Europe and America, even though the War has brought signs of change for the better.

Our situation, social and international, then, is still tense with the possibilities of disaster. Only intelligent control over the situation can avert disaster, and the first step in intelligent control is clear recognition of the mistakes of the past. The Great War came as a shock to those who had not studied intimately the foundations of nineteenth-century European civilization; but we now know that it was not an accident of any sort, in diplomacy or otherwise, but rather a natural result of the leading developments of our politics, business, and ethics of the last fifty years. The War merely exposed the rottenness of some of the foundations of our civilization. We had supposed that we could rear a secure social structure upon the basis of an egoistic and materialistic social philosophy. We thought that somehow out of a programme of self-interest, material satisfactions, and brute force, followed by men and nations, a settled and harmonious order would result. No one seemed to imagine that the "mores of barbarism," tolerated in private life, might express themselves actively in the life of the nations.

Even now there are those who fail to see that the egoistic, materialistic, imperialistic doctrines which got such a hold of Western civilization in the nineteenth century, both in theory and in practice, were the chief cause of the War and remain the main source of present disorders. They claim to find more ultimate causes in purely objective biological and economic conditions. But those who see clearly must perceive that while biological and economic conditions may act as stimuli, the immediate roots of civilization are always in the mental attitudes and conscious values of individuals. The conduct of great masses of men is determined by their "mores," that is, by the social standards set up and approved by the group; and these in turn are usually rooted in the values handed down in tradition from the past. Whether a given objective "cause" will result in war or not, will accordingly depend altogether upon the "mores" of a people. With warlike "mores," with belief in the philosophy of force and of group interest, the most trifling cause may produce a war; but with unwarlike mores no such effect is seen.[3]

Those who see that our civilization is rooted in mental attitudes and conscious values must also see that the attitudes and values handed down to us by the nineteenth century have often proved unsound in practice; that the nineteenth century really understood little of the principles of human living to-gether — of the social problem; and that it was for this reason that it failed to develop a stable civilization. The reconstruction

[3] See the writer's chapter on "The War and Social Evolution" in *America and the New Era*, edited by E. M. Friedman.

forced on us by the War demands, then, first
of all that we reëxamine our social theories;
for, as has been well said, we need not
simply a bigger house, but a better house to
live in.

We do not mean, of course, that the nineteenth century was not full of promising
movements and ideas, which constitute still
the richest part of our social heritage; but
rather merely that in certain respects it was
singularly short-sighted, particularistic, and
static in its social views. It was a struggle
for adjustment in a narrower world than
ours; but within it began that mighty struggle
between autocracy and democracy, between
barbarism and civilization, between the pagan
ideal of life with its emphasis upon force
and the Christian ideal with its emphasis
upon love, between the forces of social disorder and reaction on the one hand and of
social reconstruction and progress on the
other, which it bequeathed to us. The nineteenth century failed to resolve this conflict
because of its inadequate social knowledge

and inadequate social values. All other conflicts within our civilization are evidently but parts of this one grand conflict. No one can at the present time foresee the outcome of this conflict; but all can, at least, be intelligently informed as to its existence and know something of the power of forces arrayed on either side. We are not justified in thinking that the outcome will be a matter either of chance or of fatal necessity. Nations and civilizations, so far as the historian and the sociologist can discover, do not die natural deaths; their decadence and extinction seem to be rather the result of wrong choices, of misjudgments, especially on the part of the social élite who furnish the leaders in the fields of thought and action. If then our civilization is "at the crossroads," as a recent English writer has well said,[4] let no one suppose that the road which it will ultimately take is predetermined. That will be a matter to be decided by the amount of social intelligence and character which the

[4] Figgis, *Civilization at the Cross Roads*.

8

individuals of the present and of the immediate future can show. In proportion, in
other words, as we can get an intelligent
insight into existing social problems and an
intelligent appreciation of the individual and
social qualities needed to meet these problems,
in that proportion we may hope to control
the destiny of our civilization.

The world in which we live may justly be
regarded as a new world, transformed out of
the old by the working of forces yet imper-
fectly understood. Many new problems have
suddenly come upon us, due to the increase
of population, the increase of knowledge, the
intermingling of races and cultures, the increasing interdependence of nations, the invention of new machines, and other new
developments in industry, politics, and religion. These many problems, however, have
long been seen, even by superficial students,
to be interdependent. Back of our social
problems, we are gradually coming to realize,
there is *the* social problem, but unfortunately

we are far from agreed as yet as to what that problem is. Theorists and practical reformers alike have been too prone to see it from the little corner in which they were working. The truly broad view of the problem is scarcely to be found in the social literature of the present, unless perhaps in the pages of a few writers who apparently have no appreciable influence as yet on practical social and political leaders.

The War obscured the real nature of the social problem in many ways; but in others it clarified the issues involved. It showed that the social problem cannot be defined or understood from any point of view which is merely national. The War suddenly revealed the interdependence of national groups and the common life of humanity. The rest of the civilized world stood aghast at Germany's frank avowal of group egoism as a basis for practical living. It has suddenly become evident that the unit of our sociological thinking must be humanity. We now see that group egoism, whether of a nation, class, or race, is no lovelier than individual egoism. Again, the danger of taking some particularistic principle, like that of the biological struggle for existence,[5] from some single aspect of life, and conceiving the human problem preponderatingly in its terms, has also become evident. We are beginning to see that all the factors which shape civilized human life, whether material or immaterial, must be taken into account in any truly broad view of the social problem.

The reconstruction of our civilization, it has become evident, should not be a patchwork. It should grapple with the whole problem of our civilization — the whole social problem of the present. It should aim at the harmonious adjustment of all elements and factors in our social life, so that we should no longer have an inharmonious and divided world. But to do this we must transcend the narrow, particularistic views of the social

[5] For a flagrant example of this sort of particularism, see Bernhardi's *Germany and the Next War.*

11

problem, upon the basis of which dangerous, one-sided programmes of social reconstruction are advocated.[6]

Let us specify briefly some of the particularistic views of the social problem which are dangerously prevalent at the present time. To many, whose vision has been confined largely to the economic relations of classes within the nation, the modern social problem has seemed essentially the labour problem. If it is not merely the problem of the harmonious adjustment of employer and employee, it is at most the problem of finding a social order in which work and enjoyment shall be in satisfactory relationship to each other. Hence the generally prevalent view that the social problem is essentially the problem of the satisfactory production and just distribution of wealth. To find the proper methods of producing and distributing material goods, would solve the social problem, according to these thinkers.

[6] Compare Cooley's *Social Process*, Chap. V.

Many eugenists and feminists, on the other hand, insist that the real social problem is the problem of the control of heredity, or, of the relations of the sexes. If the proper breeding of man could be assured, or if woman could be given full freedom, that, they seem to think, would solve the essential problem of humanity.

The views of economists, eugenists, and feminists are all to be welcomed as tending to bring out the larger human elements in the problem. Some of us, at least, are beginning to perceive that the social problem is now, what it has been in all ages, namely, *the problem of the relations of men to one another.*[7] It is the problem of human living together, and cannot be confined to any statement in economic, eugenic or other one-sided terms. The social problem is neither the labour problem, nor the problem of the dis-

[7] This, of course, does not exclude the consideration of the physical environment or of subjective elements (ideas, feelings, etc.) in so far as they affect the relations of men to one another. See following chapters.

13

tribution of wealth, nor the problem of the relation of population to natural resources, nor of the control of hereditary qualities, nor of the harmonious adjustment of the relations of the sexes; but it is all of these and much more. If the social problem is the problem of human living together, then it is as broad as humanity and human nature, and no mere statement of it in terms of one set of factors will suffice. Such a statement obscures the real nature of the problem, and may lead to dangerous, one-sided attempts at its solution.

A word of caution is necessary here. Because the greatest possible broadmindedness is needful to view aright the social problem— the problem of human living together—it must not be thought that it is beyond the power of the human intellect or of science. On the contrary, we may boldly claim that if we will keep to the common-sense view of the world, and not be seduced by one-sided philosophies, enough knowledge of how human groups do actually live together has

14

already been accumulated to make it possible
for any well-trained mind to see deeply and
truly into the problem of human living together—whether the living together concern
two or three individuals or humanity as a
whole. Nor must it be thought that because
so many different factors are involved in our
social life that there is no such thing as "the
social problem," that it is only a name for
many different problems. On the contrary,
nothing is so real as the social problem—the
problem of living together. Every age, nation, and individual must solve it in some
way, by howsoever crude a social philosophy.
But to solve it aright for humanity at large—
in universal terms, so to speak—requires a
scientific understanding of the forces at work
in human interrelations, and careful putting
together in a right way of all the factors concerned. In brief, it requires a scientific
sociology.

Let us, therefore, consider the nature of the
unity of a social group in the light of modern
sociology in order to see what the nature of

the social problem of the present is upon scientific analysis.[8] A social group, whatever else it may be, is a mass of interactions between the individuals who compose it; but if it is to have any sort of unity, these interactions must be regulated and controlled, that is, the activities of the individual members of the group must be adjusted to one another in some more or less definite way. Otherwise, the group cannot work together as a unit nor can its actions work out to any definite end. While analogies are dangerous in science, it may be helpful to compare our social group to a machine. Now the unity of a machine is secured by the nice adjustment of its parts to one another. If this adjustment is not mechanically perfect, there is friction and it will not work well, or perhaps not at all. So in the social group there must be this nice adjustment between the activities of its in-

[8] For a more detailed and scientific analysis of the nature of social unity, see Chapters IV and V of the writer's *Introduction to Social Psychology* (D. Appleton & Co., 1917.)

dividual members, if the group is to work
well as a unity, or even at all. But the parts
of the social mechanism, if we may so call it,
are not bits of dead, inert physical matter,
but are living, feeling, thinking individual
units. The machinist has only to know the
principles of physics in order to manipulate
the parts of the machine as he will, to secure
its harmonious working. But the social leader
cannot so easily manipulate the individuals
of his group. He must understand human
nature in all of its phases; that is, he must
know the principles of psychology instead of
physics to make the social mechanism work
harmoniously. He must understand all the
factors, in other words, involved in that adjustment of the activities of individuals to
one another, which is necessary in order that
the group may work together as a unity.

Now the factors which are involved in the
harmonious adjustment of the parts of our
social machine are evidently very numerous.
First of all, of course, are the external physical
conditions. These must be such as to favour

the normal development of human life in all
ways or else the social machine will work
badly or not at all. But taking favourable
conditions in the external environment for
granted, it is evident that many internal
factors will need to be considered. First
among these is the biological make-up of the
individuals concerned, and the impulses or
instincts which this make-up gives rise to.
Unless these are such as to favour the adjustment of the activities of individuals concerned,
we can scarcely expect any high degree of
social unity. Heredity must be right or else
our social machine will not work well. Beyond
heredity, and practically more important, is
the matter of the acquired habits of the individuals of the group. Either these habits
must be similar, or if different, must be such
that they can be harmoniously coördinated,
or else again we will have little or no social
unity. Mere habituation has much to do
with maintaining social order; and therefore,
external circumstances which affect habit
must be strictly controlled by a group if it is to

keep its unity. But if any social unity of more than a merely animal sort is to be attained certain purely subjective elements must also be taken into account. For in all conscious human groups it is the mental attitude of the individuals towards one another which is the final, decisive factor which decides whether a group shall maintain its unity or be disrupted. There are, for example, the feelings, sentiments, ideas, beliefs, and opinions of the group. Not only must these be similar within certain limits, but the members of the group must be more or less conscious of this similarity, that is, they must develop mutual sympathy and understanding. From mutual sympathy and understanding, moreover, arise confidence and reciprocal trust which make possible still closer coördination between the members of a group.

All of these are necessary that the mechanism of human society may work harmoniously. And such facts show conclusively that the unity of human groups is essentially a psychic or spiritual matter. Destroy the psychic element in it, and we should have no society. Even if the psychic element may be only a means to perfect the adjustments of life, still it is evidently the absolutely decisive factor in the social life of civilized men. And we shall see as we proceed that the psychic or spiritual elements in social life are not wholly derived from the immediate environment, but have a life history of their own. These simple principles of social unity apply to all human groups, from the simplest to humanity if it shall ever become organized.

But what makes civilization? The level of civilization in social evolution is not reached until in addition to the instincts, habits, and feelings we have certain socially recognized values and coördinating, unifying ideas which form a social tradition. For essentially civilization is the discovery, diffusion and the transmission from age to age of the knowledge, beliefs, ideas and values by which men have found it possible to conquer nature and live together in well-ordered groups.

20

It is, in large measure, the substitution of a "subjective environment" of ideas and values for the objective environment of material objects; and cultural evolution is possible only through the continuity of this subjective environment, that is, through the continuity of ideas and social values. *Civilization, in other words, is at bottom the creation and transmission of social values by which men regulate their conduct.* It is, therefore, essentially a spiritual affair and cannot be measured by changes in the material environment, prone as we may be to measure it thus. While human society was from the start psychic, it is manifest that only in its higher developments does it become so dominated by the psychic that it may well be called spiritual. Likeness in the beliefs and ideals of its members becomes finally even more important than the likeness of impulse, habit and feeling which was the original foundation of group life.

Civilized human beings, in other words, cannot live together harmoniously without some mutually accepted scale of values by which they can measure and regulate conduct. They need not only the like-mindedness which springs from similar impulses, habits, emotions, and feelings, but also generally accepted ideas and ideals of life, if they are to achieve any social order worthy to be called civilized. A civilized social order must rest upon certain ideal values, which, at least in a democratic society, must be accepted by a large majority of the population.

Now, when we look out on Western society, we find absolute difference, if not hopeless conflict, between the fundamental beliefs and ideals of its members. If Western civilization is at present torn with conflicts, it is because just now its world of values is topsy-turvey. Faith in the old ideals by which men have lived in the past has decayed in many classes, and no new ideals have yet been found and generally accepted upon which to build a new social order.[9] There is scarcely an institu-

[9] Compare the chapter on "The Intellectual Temper of the Age" in Professor Santayana's *The Winds of*

tion from the family to the State which is not in the crucible of fiery criticism and in apparent disintegration. Take the institution of the family for illustration. Instead of the general acceptance of permanent monogamy as the ideal of the family, which it was until very recently in Western civilization, we now see this form of the family attacked on every side by groups which advocate divorce by mutual consent, free love, polygamy, and even promiscuity. The proportion of individuals who hold to these views in Western civilization is now so great that their existence can no longer be ignored, while it must be admitted that an even larger number practise these theories without being willing to admit that they hold them as their standards. In other words, much of the present criticism of the family is no longer constructive, but is anarchistic and absolutely destructive, and is proving so in actual practice.

Doctrine—a book which itself especially well illustrates the fact that in many fundamental beliefs the modern world is still "in full career toward disintegration."

Again, if we take literature prior to the War as reflecting the inner condition of our civilization, the absolute disagreement as to ideals of life becomes even more plainly visible. A very large part of pre-war literature repudiated not only the traditional standards of Christian ethics, but all truly humanitarian standards whatsoever. It exalted the individual as an end and as a law unto himself, and not infrequently inculcated the gratification of natural impulses and appetites as the highest good in life. It often derided the ideals of service and of self-sacrifice for the sake of service, and even the idea of social obligation. The individual and his feelings were its supreme value. It was not simply a few minor writers who thus flouted the traditional morality of Christendom in the family and in general social relations, but some of the foremost figures in literature. The decay of our moral ideals was evident, then, from even a cursory acquaintance with modern literature.

There is much other evidence to show that

for two or three decades prior to the War the standards, attitudes, and values characteristic of barbarism [10] showed signs of reviving in Western civilization. This was to be seen not merely in the literature and art of the period, but especially in its politics, business, and ideals of life. Power and force became exalted, and "success" often the only recognized standard. Gradually the various groups of Western civilization drew apart into hostile camps and the appeal of certain elements was more and more to force. Conciliation and goodwill were stigmatized as mere weakness, and peace was sought only in a balance of egoisms, that is, in a balance of power, of armaments, and of selfish interests. The

[10] Barbarism is that stage in the development of culture, between savagery and true civilization, which is particularly characterized by the rule of force. Militancy and predatoriness were the chief traits of barbarism, and out of them grew its typical institutions, such as slavery, autocracy, fixed social castes, polygamy, etc. Most of these institutions survive in early civilization, and indeed some of them we are but just getting rid of.

doctrine of the "big stick" became popular.
Power politics (*Machtpolitik*) were held to be
the only practical sort. Worse yet, predatory
business practices came to be countenanced
increasingly among certain elements in an
economic system avowedly based upon self-
interest, while these same elements prosti-
tuted governments to the end that they
might dominate the world's markets. In all
of these developments Western civilization
was reverting toward barbarism, for it was
deserting the basis of higher civilization,
which is in mutual goodwill, understanding,
and coöperation not less than in increased
knowledge; and so it was moving toward an unstable social and international
order.

All of these tendencies, though more or less
prevalent everywhere in our civilization, came
to a head in the autocratic, militaristic German state. There the worship of militarism
and Machiavellian politics, of material power
and commercial success, gradually corrupted
a whole people once famed for their social

idealism and Christian piety.[11] When Bernhardi declared [12] that "Christian morality is
personal . . . and in its nature cannot be
political," he but reëchoed a proposition
which had been affirmed by practically every
German professor of politics for two generations.[13] It was no wonder that the German people from Nietzsche down came to
believe that "Might is at once the supreme
right."

But these tendencies only *came to a head in
Germany;* for Machiavellian politics, predatory business, and the power ideal of life
were in abundant evidence in other nations
also of Western civilization. Indeed, Germany only illustrated the reversion toward
barbarism in Western civilization generally.
The Great War itself showed how little re-

[11] See Chapters II and III of Professor Ely's *World
War and Leadership in a Democracy* for a description
of the deterioration of Germany.

[12] *Germany and the Next War,* p. 29.

[13] Treitschke, *Politics.* For a less notorious example,
see von Rümelin's *Reden und Aufsätze,* Vol. I, pp. 144–
171.

moved from barbarism were the nations of
Christendom, for the most distressing thing
about the War was not its destruction of life
and property, frightful as that was, but the
barbarous hatred developed by the contending nations toward one another—a hatred
without precedent since the religious wars of
the sixteenth century. Toward the close of
the War, this hatred manifested itself not
infrequently between the classes within the
nations, showing upon how slender a basis of
understanding and goodwill in many cases
even national existence itself rested. Manifestly as long as goodwill continues to be
lacking between classes and nations, the
world must remain in an unstable condition.
How permanent world peace is to issue from
the present atmosphere of suspicion and hate
which now enshrouds the classes, nations
and races of the world is difficult for even the
wisest man to see.

Progress still halts between the ideals of
a society based upon force and of a society
based upon goodwill and rationality. If we

are going to rebuild our civilization, however, we must know what ideal we are going to build toward. We must come to some agreement as regards fundamental social values and ideals. Even the people of the United States, most fortunately situated of modern nations in many ways, were, at least prior to the War, in utter disagreement regarding fundamental social ideals. At the outbreak of the War the *American Journal of Sociology* [14] undertook to get from a number of leading Americans their opinions on "What is Americanism?" The result astonishingly demonstrated the lack of like-mindedness among the American people as to the ideals which should guide their future civilization. The editor, Professor Small, remarked: "The one illustrative value (of the symposium) to which we call attention is the exhibit of the miscellaneousness of American minds." The unity of action demanded by the exigencies of war tended, of course, in some measure to correct temporarily this "miscellaneousness

[14] Vol. XX, pp. 433–486 (January, 1915).

of minds" in America, as well as in other
countries. There was during the war especially a great deal of lip service of democracy, but there is still lacking evidence
to show that Americans are united on the
great questions concerning government, industry, the family, education, and moral
ideals.

It may be worth while here to quote the
opinion of Ferrero, careful student of both
classic antiquity and of contemporary social
conditions. "We are travelling," he tells us,
"step by step back toward paganism, with all
of its inconveniences and all its perils." Confusion with reference to the ideals of life and
tendencies toward barbarism, or "paganism,"
in Western civilization, however, have appeared in menacing strength only within
comparatively recent years. They do not
necessarily mean social degeneration; they
may mean only temporary social deterioration.
But they make our age one of peculiar peril,
for reasons which we shall see, and the problem
of social reconstruction more than the mere

superficial one of making a few political and economic changes.

These statements are not made, then, as a basis for any pessimistic conclusion. They are given simply as facts. Such facts are indications, to be sure, of grave social disorder; but such disorder, may, to a certain extent, be a normal accompaniment of the profound social changes through which Western civilization is now passing.[15] To be sure, the negative social ideas which now prevail among certain classes in Western nations cannot be considered an indication of social normality. On the contrary, they present real dangers; but our contention is that in passing from one type of social order to another we must expect a certain amount of confusion in regard to the ideas and ideals by which men govern their lives. It is impossible for societies to change their methods of living without some degree of confusion, just as it is impossible for individuals to make such changes without some confu-

[15] See writer's *Sociology in Its Psychological Aspects*, pp. 173, 178 (D. Appleton & Co.).

sion.[16] Now, when the change which has to
be made is a great one, there will be more opportunity for such confusion. If societies
could keep a high degree of flexibility in their
institutions, intelligently changing them to
meet all changing conditions, there probably
never would be any such thing as the breakdown of institutions or social order. In other
words, there would never be any social revolutions. There would be only gradual social
evolution. Unfortunately, however, the ruling classes of a society rarely keep the flexibility and plasticity in institutions which
they should ideally possess. Through shortsightedness or personal interest they attempt
to block normal social changes, and that is the
way largely that trouble begins in civilized
societies. In reaction from the conservatism
of the ruling classes dangerous forms of radicalism with socially negative and disintegrating
ideas emerge. These disintegrating ideas are
used as weapons to attack the existing order of
society. The revolt against the existing order

[16] See *Sociology in Its Psychological Aspects*, p. 173.

spreads to all the classes unfavourably affected by existing institutions, and through sympathy finally to many others. Unless the ruling classes yield, a bloody conflict between classes breaks out and we have a revolution.

If the normal course of social evolution is checked, then the stream of progress, blocked for a time by the shortsightedness or selfishness of individuals, will sooner or later break the artificial dam obstructing its path, probably with catastrophic violence, leaving social ruin and the desolation behind it. This is the essence of our theory of social revolutions: [17] and it suffices to explain the general facts of such social calamities from the French Revolution to the recent Russian and Mexican Revolutions.

Here we notice a peculiar fact about our social machine. Unlike any other machine it will not stay "put." No matter how nicely its parts may have been adjusted to one an-

[17] See Chapter VIII of the writer's *Introduction to Social Psychology* for a more detailed exposition.

other through some cleverly devised social system, say, through the unifying effect of some generally accepted social policy, they cannot remain adjusted on this plane long; for the conditions of life change, and the social order which worked well yesterday will no longer work to-day. In matters of social organization it is preëminently true that "time makes ancient good uncouth." Civilized human societies must be, therefore, in a continuous process of readjustment. Progress is the very law of their being: and if the ruling classes in any society attempt to enforce a policy of standing still, there is bound to be trouble. The only way to avert social revolution, as Turgot declares, is through suitable and well-timed reforms. The surest way to bring on a revolution, on the other hand, is for the ruling classes to attempt to preserve an order of society which no longer works well; and if we may judge from the lack of adaptability and of intelligent sense of social responsibility of some who are in power in American industry, law, and government, the outlook is bad for American society just at the present moment.

But if confusion as regards the ideals of life is normal in periods of social transition,[18] and if some development of purely negative or destructive radicalism is to be expected at such times as a natural reaction from the ultra-conservatism of the ruling classes, where is the danger? The reply is that the danger consists in this social confusion and disintegration going too far. There is no assurance in either history or sociology of continuous progressive evolution, that is, there is no assurance that when institutions break down they will be replaced by better adapted or higher institutions. On the contrary, there is always the danger that there will be a reversion to a lower type of social order and of civilization. Socially negative and disintegrating doctrines may be first elaborated as weapons of attack against some existing in-

[18] *Sociology in Its Psychological Aspects*, pp. 173, 174, 176, 177.

stitution, which is no longer adapted, but the fury of party fanaticism may lead them to be taken as adequate doctrines in themselves. The result is seen in the tendency toward anarchy frequently manifested in revolutionary periods, in the series of profound social disorders, culminating finally in the appearance of "the strong man" who is invoked to restore order by despotic means.

Let us recall again the nature of civilization, that it consists essentially in the propagation and conservation of certain ideal social values. We see immediately that civilization is from its very nature a fragile affair: that it is possible for any of the great value traditions of civilized society to be broken down at any moment, especially those which have respect to the higher institutions and relationships. And as Hobhouse says, "If the tradition [19] is broken, the race begins again

[19] Tradition, in the sociological sense, includes all knowledge, belief, ideals, standards and values handed down from the past. Its influence upon the individual may be, of course, either *conscious* or *unconscious*.

where it stood before the tradition was formed."[20] It is easily possible, in other words, for civilized societies to return to barbarism,[21] though a complete return would perhaps necessitate centuries in the case of high civilizations, since not all civilizing traditions could be broken down at once. This process of the decay of the higher social values may, of course, go on in times of social peace through the undermining of the sense of social obligation and social responsibility by materialism and individualism; and we have seen it long going on among ourselves. But in periods of international war and of internal revolution,

---

[20] *Social Evolution and Political Theory*, p. 39.

[21] It may be reasonably argued that retrogressive movements are more liable to take place in high civilizations than in low ones on account of the delicacy of the structure of the higher civilization. Again, war has become so much more destructive, affects so much more national and international life, that the effects of a prolonged war among Western nations might be to set civilization back centuries. We are not justified in concluding, therefore, that modern civilization is more stable than ancient civilization.

with their bloody conflicts between peoples and classes, the process of social disintegration and of relapse towards barbarism may be infinitely accelerated. For in such conflicts the animal instincts of man are frightfully stimulated and apt to gain control, while negative social doctrines, becoming the watchwords of parties, are made the impossible foundations of social order. Where such conflicts are long continued, the social loss and damage must soon become irreparable.

It is not difficult to see the application of such facts to the doctrine now growing in popularity among us that we must expect social progress by revolution, just as we have organic evolution by mutation. It is true that social progress has often come by revolution in the past, but usually also at fearful social cost. An actual bloody conflict between classes cannot occur without social ruin and disaster. If the wounds of such conflicts as the French Revolution and the American Civil War have healed, owing to the recupera-

tive power of our civilization, this method of
progress is certainly too costly for any civilized people to tolerate. If social science cannot show us a better way of progress than by
revolution, it is the most useless of disciplines.
For we need not only right aims in social
change but we must employ wise methods
as well; otherwise our methods may defeat
our aims. The method of revolution is particularly objectionable in social change since it
is doubly liable to defeat its aim. On the one
hand, through the bloody conflicts which it
may involve, it may do irreparable injury
to the finer traditions of civilization; on the
other, through the persistence of habit, it is
especially liable to be followed by reaction.

Enough perhaps has been said about the
nature of society and of social changes to
show the essentially psychic or spiritual
nature of the whole modern social problem;
that it is primarily a problem of values, of
ideals, of opinions as to human living together. This is, indeed, in practice admitted

by all except a few fatalists or mechanists.
Practical socialists and eugenists, for example,
are as busy trying to straighten out our values
as to human living as the old time moralists
and theologians ever were. The chief difference is that some socialists and some eugenists
seem to think that if our values as to economic or biological conditions are straightened
out, all other values will spontaneously right
themselves. They seem to say that the conditions under which men do their work are
so all-important that if they are rightly controlled the conditions of their leisure and
amusements will need no control; or that
hereditary qualities are so important that if
they are properly controlled we need not
concern ourselves very greatly about the
influence of the environment. There is tremendous one-sidedness in many of the social
programmes of to-day; but all parties are practically agreed as to the need of influencing
the opinions and beliefs of a considerable
element of the population before desired social
changes can be brought about.

But to say that the social problem of the present day is essentially spiritual is not to deny the presence in it of many non-spiritual factors. *Man's social life, like individual character, develops about two poles—one the material conditions of life, and the other the psychic controls over life, which are represented by values, ideas and ideals.*[22] No one who has investigated the social conditions of the present would deny for one instant the importance of the material conditions of life, especially of economic conditions, upon our civilization; and of late we are beginning to appreciate, owing to the labours of eugenists and social workers, the importance among the material conditions of the biological element also. But, admitting the importance of the material conditions of life, the attack upon the problems which they present must come in the first instance through bringing to bear upon them our ideas, ideals, and valuations; and this is merely equivalent to saying that our ideas, ideals, and values must be so ex-

[22] *Cf.* Ross, *Foundations of Sociology*, p. 230.

panded that they include, and give adequate recognition to these material elements.

But, when we say that the social problem is essentially spiritual, something more is meant than that it must be attacked by intellectual processes—by science—if it is to be solved. What is meant is that the psychic elements in it are so influential and so independent that they must be considered preponderant. We mean, in other words, that the ideas and ideals of our present civilization have had a life history of their own, not to be understood through the study of material conditions alone; that there is continuity on the spiritual as well as on the material side in social conditions; and that it *is the conflict between inharmonious traditions and ideals in our culture, on the one hand, and the lack of adaptation of our ideas and ideals to the present conditions of life, on the other, which have produced the modern social problem.* Whether we look at the problem from the standpoint of the blindness of our ruling classes, or from the standpoint of the hatred and malice of some of the non-privileged; whether we consider the decay of the family or the deterioration of our racial stock; whether we regard the conflicts between individuals or between nations, *what is visible everywhere are confused, inadequate, conflicting ideas and ideals of life*. Men are in inharmonious relations, classes and nations are in conflict, civilization is rent asunder in the modern world, because men have been trying to live by socially inadequate, conflicting, one-sided ideas and values.

The nineteenth century, as we have seen, sowed and nourished the seeds of both world war and world revolution. It is time that we recognize the rotten stones that have been laid in the foundations of Western civilization; for these must be removed if the whole superstructure is not to fall. We have been trying to build a delicate and complex social structure upon inadequate and even negative social ideas and values. As examples, we need only point to the materialism, individualism, exaggerated nationalism, imperialism, and class egoism of the nineteenth century, which the twentieth century also is apparently starting out to take as its practical guides. These doctrines are socially negative: materialism, because at bottom it denies the reality of the spiritual values which alone make civilization possible; individualism, because it denies the reality of the common life, upon recognition of which must rest the sense of social responsibility and obligation; exaggerated nationalism, or national egoism, because it denies the reality of the common life of humanity and the unlimited obligation of nations to humanity. From such national egoism has sprung directly those imperialistic ambitions which menace the peace of nations; while class egoism is obviously but a manifestation of the same spirit of group egoism in the life of a smaller group. Yet these socially negative and destructive doctrines are so embedded in the structure of our civilization that their most prominent advocates are often found among our intellectual and social élite.

In such a civilization, with such an environment of socially negative, one-sided, and conflicting ideals and values, it is not to be wondered at that we are producing so many distorted and socially negative characters, such as anarchists, Bolshevists, I. W. W.'s, and other advocates of violence in dealing with social questions. Our civilization has evidently been breeding within itself a mass of barbarians who do not respect its higher values. These are the only enemies of which it has need to be afraid; for Western civilization is no longer seriously threatened by external foes. If its walls are ever pulled down it will not be by the barbarians of Africa or Asia, but by the barbarians within its gates. Only recently, has humanity come to a place in its long march up the slopes of progress where it can see an apparently clear road ahead. But it has scarcely achieved this when enemies within its own ranks seem about to obstruct and hamper its march.

Yet the situation calls for no pessimism, but only alertness and intelligent appreciation of real dangers and difficulties, and on the part of social leaders a genuine largeness of mind in seeing all the factors involved. Western civilization needs a great social and spiritual awakening. Its whole atmosphere must be changed. Justice must be established between man and man in economic and other relations of life; and the tradition of peace must be established among the nations. Finally, the springs of individual character must be controlled, so that civilization can get rid of the stragglers, the hangers-on, and the enemies that obstruct its march. To admit that the social problem depends at all for its solution upon the control of individual character has seemed to many to admit the hopelessness of the problem; but we hope to show that this is a mistake, and that wise social leadership is all that is needed to deal with even this most difficult aspect of our problem.[23]

[23] For a detailed study of social leadership, see Chapters VIII–X of Ely's *World War and Leadership in a Democracy.*

Our present social situation, then, instead of leading to a counsel of despair, should be an inspiration to effort; for social self-determinism is no mere idle dream of closet philosophers. It is a demonstrated fact of experience as well as a programme built upon the understanding of sociological truth. Human society is but entering upon the self-conscious phase of its own evolution. Through consciousness of its own condition, it can, if it will, control its own destiny, though not in any arbitrary way. The question before us is whether we shall abandon the policy of social drifting, which has hitherto characterized our civilization, and enter upon a policy of mastery over the conditions of our social existence. But before there can be mastery, there must first be a scientific understanding on the part of social leaders of the part played by each factor which enters into our civilization and which may make or mar its future. It is the purpose of the next five chapters to make clear the part played by each of the principal factors.

47

CHAPTER II

HISTORICAL ELEMENTS IN THE MODERN SOCIAL PROBLEM

TRADITION plays a great part in the development of human society. Knowledge, ideas, and valuations, handed down from generation to generation, make the continuity of the social life on its spiritual side.[24] They largely make the social environment of the developing individual, and so largely control his social development. Tradition thus enters into every social situation. The economic determinists to the contrary notwithstanding, the spiritual elements in human society have a history of their own. That history is so important that no problem in existing social life can be understood apart

[24] For an admirable discussion of the importance of "tradition" in the social life, see Hobhouse, *Social Evolution and Political Theory*, pp. 33–38.

from its rootage in social tradition. This it is which makes history one of the chief methods of the social sciences. Until we know something of the history of the ideas and ideals which make our civilization what it is, it is fatuous to think that we have any scientific understanding of the social problem of the present.

It is not our purpose, however, in attempting some slight analysis of the traditional elements which enter into our problem, to go back to the very beginnings of human history, even though it were possible to do so. Doubtless it is within the fields of cultural anthropology and primitive history that the earliest beginnings of the things which we are about to discuss must be sought. It would not be difficult, for example, to show how man, as he has gradually risen into the higher stages of culture, has carried with him many of the traditions of the savage and barbarian periods of development. In a sense, civilization is still very young. Even in the material things of life man left the stone age behind but yesterday, while in spiritual things he still lingers in it. The social and moral traditions of savagery and barbarism, in other words, still survive among us. They are not only a source of maladjustments and evils in present society, but, aided by the animal instincts of human nature, they forever threaten to carry us back to the barbarism from which we have but just emerged. If we are to build a true civilization, we must get rid of the "mores of barbarism" still lingering among us; for as long as they are held in honor, strife for mere power will continue to divide our world.

This feature of the social problem, however, we do not propose here to discuss. Our purpose in the present chapter is rather to make an analysis of the immediate sources of Western civilization; to find out what its immediate predecessors have contributed to it, and what new forces it has generated within itself.

We must remember, first of all, that Western

civilization is a hybrid affair; that it is made up of elements derived from many sources. We are frequently told that modern civilization is a continuation of the civilization of Greece and Rome, and this, we shall see, is true in no superficial sense. However, the cultures of two other ancient peoples have profoundly affected our own. These peoples were the Hebrews and the ancient Teutonic tribes. From the Hebrews, indeed, we get the things most intimately connected with our social ideals—our ethics and our religion. Nominally, at least, Western civilization accepts Hebrew ethics and religion still to-day as its standard, though there are not wanting signs which indicate that whole classes in our population are on the point of throwing off even nominal allegiance to this standard.

Whatever the scientific student of culture may think of Hebrew ethics and religion, he must acknowledge the conquest of the Western world by Hebrew ethical and religious ideas and ideals to be one of the most wonderful phenomena of recorded history. The Western world did not accept the God of the Jews because the Jews held any sort of material or spiritual supremacy in the ancient world. It is notorious that they were a feeble and despised people. Some historians and social philosophers have sought to explain the spread of their religious and ethical ideas by supposing that these ideas became greatly modified, if not entirely changed, through contact with Greek civilization; and that it was the Greek element in Christianity which really made it acceptable to the Western world. Without entering upon this controversy, it will suffice for our purpose to point out that modern scholarship finds nothing in the teachings of Jesus which is not to be found implicit, at least, in the teachings of the later Jewish prophets.[25] This Jesus himself recognized. His work must, indeed, be considered the logical culmination of their work. If we distinguish Christianity sharply from the dogmas that

[25] Professor Santayana aptly characterizes the teaching of Jesus as "pure Hebraism reduced to its spiritual essence." *Reason and Religion*, p. 84.

early grew up within the Church, the relation of Christianity to Judaism will be seen to be not different from that of the full-blown rose to its bud.[26] The Græco-Roman world doubtless furnished the proper environmental conditions which favoured this development, but when we analyze the teachings of Jesus, we find them Jewish to the core, even though they had burst the bonds of Jewish particularism. Hebrew religion and ethics thus became nominally accepted by the Western world with the acceptance of Christianity.

There seems to be but one rational explanation of the spread of these Jewish ideas, and that is, the transcendent genius of the ancient Jews in ethical and religious matters.[27] As

[26] The work of the "apocalyptic" scholars, such as Dr. R. H. Charles of Oxford, has shown that there were no "silent centuries" between the Old and the New Testaments, but continuous development. See Charles, *Between the Old and the New Testaments*.

[27] "Ethical" and "religious" are, of course, here used in their specialized sense, not as including the legal, the political, the intellectual, the artistic, etc.

one writer has put it, "They alone were sober, when all the other nations of the world were drunk." Their ethical and religious conceptions have conquered the world because of their inherent truthfulness and social usefulness. Let it be remarked that it is no more absurd to acknowledge the preëminence of the Hebrews along ethical and religious lines than to acknowledge the preëminence of the Greeks along artistic lines. Ethics and religion are indeed much more intimately related to life and conduct than art. The values which they represent have more immediate relation to everyday social life. Because they are so necessary for social survival and development, it does not surprise the student of social evolution to find that ethical and religious concepts should have attained a high development earlier than scientific or even artistic ideas.

Just why this high development of ethical and religious concepts took place among the Jews rather than among some other ancient people is not difficult to understand as soon as we consider their social life. When the Jews first appeared in history, probably no less than a full millennium of Semitic civilization already lay behind them.[28] They were perhaps able to profit from the mistakes of their Semitic predecessors, as their own writers so often inform us. They developed a simple, pastoral life in which the patriarchal family was the unit of their society. Many writers, following Renan, have ascribed Jewish monotheism to their geographic environment; but it is not too much to say that such a theory is absurd. As soon as we consider their social organization, and especially the part which the family played in that organization, the reasons for their ethical and religious conceptions become clear.[29] All their religious and ethical concepts are based upon the family,

[28] See Professor J. L. Myres' *Dawn of History*, Chapter V.

[29] For the ideas in the remainder of this paragraph the writer is indebted to Professor J. F. MacCurdy's work: *History, Prophecy and the Monuments, or Israel among the Nations*, Vol. II, especially Chapters II and III.

and are really at bottom merely an idealization and projection of the values connected with the family life. God was thought of by them as a father, men as his children, and therefore brothers. All the phraseology of the later prophets especially was borrowed from the domestic and social life. It was, in a word, the superior unity and harmony of the social life of the ancient Jews, especially of their family life, which produced their superior ethical and religious conceptions. As a consequence, both their ethics and religion were preëminently social, even though at first narrowly national. They thought of the moral ideal, not as something subjective and individualistic, but as the harmony of an ideal social group, especially as the love and service of an enlarged family. When these conceptions were universalized by the later prophets and by Jesus, they became social in a broader sense, that is, humanitarian.[30] Social develop-

[30] For the full justification of this preliminary identification of the ethics of Jesus and humanitarian ethics, see the later pages of this Chapter and also

ments in the Græco-Roman world had in the meantime done much to prepare the world for the acceptance of such ideas and ideals, and hence they were the more readily taken up by the whole Western world.

To put it from a somewhat different standpoint, the peculiar merit of Jewish ethics was that it blended religion and morality, resting both of these upon an ideal projection of the values of the family life. This gave a deeper meaning to morality and religion as well as to the social life. At first the resulting moral conceptions were doubtless crude and narrow; but gradually through the course of Hebrew history they become more spiritual, and, at length, were universalized in the later prophets and in Christianity. On the other hand, the religion of the Greeks was so nearly unmoral that their ethical leaders, Socrates and Plato, saw no chance of promoting ideal social ethics through Greek religion. The divorce of ethics from religion seemed to them absolutely neces-

Chapter V. Christianity as a religion is, of course, something more than mere humanitarianism.

sary for the progress of morality. But the later religionless systems of Greek ethics proved largely sterile, for they became current only to a limited degree or in degraded forms. Thus Jewish ethics, combining the theistic and the moral ideas—thus kindling morality with religious emotion—and resting both upon the social life, was alone among ancient systems fitted to survive and to spread over Western civilization, though this was facilitated by the existence of such systems as Platonism and Stoicism.

Now, if it is true that we have received our religious and ethical standards from the ancient Jews, then we must no longer give the Greeks the place of honour for having made the most important contribution to Western civilization, but must give that place to the Hebrews. For, as we have implied, religion and ethics so intimately embody the ideals and values of social life that they must be considered the chief carriers of civilization. Hebrew religion and ethics did not, however, find a clear field. In expanding, these creations of Hebrew culture entered a world filled with many hostile traditions and with many practices that were entirely inconsistent with their principles. Hebrew civilization, therefore, contributed but one element, though a very important one, in our civilization. From the first, the other elements in Western civilization have threatened to engulf the Jewish ethical and religious tradition.

While we cannot regard the Greeks as having made the most important contribution to Western civilization, we must acknowledge that Greek traditions have in many ways been very influential. In two lines of human activity—the artistic and the philosophic—they were as preëminent as the Hebrews in religion and ethics, and have set the standard for the modern world. The Greeks must be especially credited with intellectual and æsthetic genius. In art not only were they preëminent among ancient peoples, but their artistic sense dominated their whole life. This is the secret at once of the strength and the weakness of the Greek ideal of life. They saw everything

in terms of beauty. Their religion was a
religion of beauty; and their ethics partook of
the same character. Their ideal of life was,
in a word, to be "artists in living."

Greek ethics, accordingly, was largely subjective and individualistic in character.[31] To
be sure, the best of their ethical thought was
essentially social, as Plato's development of
the idea of justice in the *Republic*. But the
ethical ideals of Plato, Aristotle and even
the later Stoics, as we have seen, appealed
only to the select few. The Sophists and the
Epicureans, on the other hand, who must
be regarded as, on the whole, truly voicing
the Greek ideal of life, put forth essentially

[31] "Individualistic" in the sense that they thought
of the criterion of conduct as *within* the individual,
whereas the Hebrews thought of the criterion of conduct as quite objective to the individual—"in the will
of God." Systems of subjective ethics are, of course,
to be found at a much earlier date in India, but these
did not affect Western civilization. The usual statement found in text books that Greek ethics were objective in character is based upon a somewhat one-sided
view of the systems of Plato and Aristotle.

individualistic ethical ideals. They taught an ethics of self-realization, asserting either that self-development was the goal of life or that individual happiness was the *summum bonum*, both agreeing that enlightened self-interest was the guide of life. Individualistic and subjective standards in ethics, therefore, originated with the Greeks, and the total influence of Greek ethical tradition upon our own has been to exalt the self-culture and happiness ideals of life. How these ideals worked out in Greek society itself, history fully records. Almost from the first Grecian civilization was corrupt, and at length in certain of its features it became degraded beyond belief.[32]

Yet Greek ethical ideals have had a profound influence upon the modern world.

[32] For the opposite view of Greek history, see A. E. Zimmern's *The Greek Commonwealth.* This writer's glorification of Greek society, however, is hardly borne out by the later developments of Greek history, and is, indeed, obtained only by glossing over the patent defects of Greek character.

This has been partly due to the tradition that classical culture must be made the foundation of all our higher education in college and university; but even more it has been due to the fact that modern philosophy has constantly turned back to Greek philosophy for inspiration and guidance. Traditionally ethics in the modern world has been a part of philosophy, and modern philosophy finds itself rooted in Greek philosophy. It is not surprising, therefore, that our educated classes have quite as often followed after the Greek ideal of life as after the Hebrew-Christian ideal. However, as we shall see later, the fact that large masses in present society are more held by the Græco-Roman ideal of life than by the Hebrew-Christian, is to be explained, perhaps, not so much through the influence of tradition, or even through the example set by many in the cultured classes, as through original human nature and the immediate conditions of modern life.

To the Greeks, too, we must not forget we owe the beginnings of the scientific investigation of nature and of human society. That freedom of the intellect which is necessary for the development of speculative thought and scientific research first found extensive realization in Greek society. The philosophic-scientific tradition was, then, firmly established in Western civilization by the Greeks, and to them those who have been concerned with the development of that tradition have ever turned for renewal of inspiration. This was, perhaps, the greatest of all the contributions of the Greeks to modern civilization, although their art reached relatively a much higher level of development than their science and philosophy.

We owe to the Greeks, then, our artistic and intellectual traditions in Western civilization; and, incidentally, through these Greek influence has had not a little to do with our ethics and our social life generally. Another ancient people, however, gave us our traditions in government and law. That people was the Romans, who, on account of their extensive conquests, were compelled to develop the machinery of government and law to a point which the world had never before known. Essentially a military and warlike people, with their standards in ethics, religion, philosophy, and art but little developed above the level of barbarism, their genius for political and legal organization laid the foundations for all modern government and legal institutions. To see how extensively Roman tradition affects government at the present time, we have only to note how the names of rulers and officials are still those which Rome gave. Roman law, though relatively late in its full development, has been the wonder and admiration of all the carefully trained lawyers in the modern world, and, as is well known, the legal systems of many countries of continental Europe still rest directly upon the Roman code. While in English-speaking countries legal systems and institutions are supposed to rest upon a more or less mythical English Common Law,[33]

[33] The term "mythical" is applied to the English Common Law to which modern courts and jurists so

yet there can be no doubt that the axioms, principles, and forms of Roman law have also powerfully influenced the law of English-speaking peoples. In this way Rome gave to the modern world the governmental and legal framework of its institutional and social life.

On the other hand, the very fact that Rome was a militant and conquering nation, aiming at the domination by force of all the known world, has been responsible for some of the most unfortunate traditions in Western civilization. Modern militaristic and imperialistic traditions represent a direct continuity with those of Rome. The keeping of standing armies, for example, was first advocated in modern times by Machiavelli, in the sixteenth century, because of his admiration of the methods of Rome. Again, the modern idea of ceaseless expansion as the condition of national life and health was a conclusion which Machiavelli drew directly from his study of Roman history. Even

often make appeal. There actually existed, of course, a body of Anglo-Saxon customs and traditions.

Nietzsche, with his doctrine that "might is right," received his inspiration far more from his classical studies than from any misinterpretation of Darwinism. The Roman Empire rested essentially upon the predatory use of brute force, upon the subjugation and exploitation of weaker peoples, with scarcely anything beyond the merely selfish aim of world dominion. It may well be doubted whether any set of traditions in the modern world has caused so much human misery and suffering as the Roman tradition. At any rate, Greece, with its sensuous æstheticism, and Rome, with its brutal, predatory militarism, have been prime corrupters of modern civilization—apart, of course, from any consideration of the brute-like instincts of human nature and the survival of the traditions of barbarism among all peoples.

But still another ancient people must be mentioned as having made at least a considerable contribution to the original traditions of Western civilization. This people was the ancient Germans. It has been said that they contributed nothing to modern civilization except the men and women who developed it. However, this seems to the writer a mistake. One strong tradition among us is certainly rooted in the life of the ancient Teutonic tribesmen; and that is the tradition of individual liberty. The North Europeans for many reasons never developed in antiquity highly organized authoritative societies, but remained largely in a state of primitive democracy with simple industries and little slavery. The tradition of individual liberty among them was accordingly kept very strong and was, according to all observers, one of their chief traits. Although later these Teutonic tribesmen were subjected to Roman authority, yet there is abundant evidence in both early German and early English history to show that the tradition of individual liberty continued among them practically uninterrupted; and to the continuance of this tradition among us we owe many of the outstanding features of Western civilization. It is largely at the basis, for example, of that ideal of a free social life which has been one of the distinguishing traits of the civilization of the English-speaking peoples, and which has come to be shared by the great majority of Western peoples.

But if the Teutonic tradition of individual liberty is responsible for much of the best in the development of modern civilization, it is equally certain that in some ways it has been extremely detrimental. The level of culture in the early Germanic tribesmen was extremely low. They were often pirates and freebooters. Their tradition of liberty was mixed up with predatory customs, and it has remained so to this day. It is not simply the biological fact that we of North European blood are descendants of pirate ancestors which makes our civilization of a more or less ruthless character, but even more the spiritual fact that we have preserved from primitive times the tradition of might being right, and of predatory individual habits. The Teutonic love of liberty, in other words, has tended at times to become a tradition of individual license.

At this point, perhaps, the reader may ex-

pect a lengthy discussion of the influence of
the rise of Christianity upon Western civilization. But as we have already shown, Christianity, in the sense of the teachings of Jesus,
must be regarded essentially as a development
of Hebrew culture, in contact, of course, with
other surrounding cultures, especially the
Græco-Roman. However, at the time of Jesus'
birth, Hebrew ethics, religion, and social life,
were far from realizing the teachings of the
later prophets, but had actually tended to
degenerate, both Church and State being in
the hands of powerful reactionary parties.
Jewish particularism and formalism again
made their appearance and cast their blighting
influence upon ethics and religion. But the
soul of Jesus rose superior to this ebb-tide in
national religion and morals. Instead of going
with the current, he boldly set his face against
it, and proclaimed himself the Messiah fore-
told by the prophets, sent to redeem Israel and
to establish her spiritual supremacy among
the nations. He preached the coming of a
social order in which God's will should be real-

ized, the "Kingdom of God"; and revolution-
ized social ethics by declaring that the service
of God consisted in the service of humanity.
Jesus and his followers among the Jews must,
therefore, be regarded as heading a progressive
movement in Jewish civilization which, while
it pointed back to the tradition of the later
prophets, looked forward to the carrying of
their ethical and religious ideals to all the nations of the earth. So, too, the early Christian
Church must be regarded largely as a social
reform party within the Roman Empire, where
Stoicism and Epicureanism at their best had
failed to mitigate the increasing inhumanities
of a complex civilization resting upon brute-
force and the predatory exploitation of classes
and peoples.

We must regard Christianity, then, as an
expansion of the Hebrew tradition, one which
burst the shell of Jewish hyper-nationalism
and made its message one to humanity as a
whole. In this process the concepts and values
of Jewish religion and ethics inevitably became universalized and humanized, but they

remained, nevertheless, essentially Jewish. We should not forget, however, that it was the transcendent personality of Jesus which made possible this marvellous result. Nothing great is achieved in human society, as we have already said, without personal leadership; and this is only one illustration out of many which might be selected from history to show how traditions become intensified and transformed, either idealized or degraded, by passing through some masterful personality. The creative influence of personality can never be safely left out of account in sociology therefore, even though for the sake of brevity we may often have to omit explicit reference to it in discussing large historical movements. It is not inconsistent to say, then, that while the influence of Christianity as a system of ideals in Western civilization is largely the continued influence of Hebrew tradition, it is also the continued influence of the personality of Jesus.

It ought to be needless to remark that the traditions of the four ancient civilizations just discussed, which have formed the basis of our own, have not always harmoniously blended. Hebrew ethics and religion have not always fitted in well with Greek philosophy and art, Roman government and law, and Teutonic individualism. Indeed, the conflict of ideas and ideals in modern life springs in no small measure from these inharmonious traditions which were originally united to form the main current of European civilization. To be sure, it was the task of the Middle Ages to blend and synthesize into an harmonious whole these varying traditions. Under the leadership of the medieval Church, Hebrew religion, Greek philosophy, and Roman government and law were in one way or another made to work peaceably together, while Teutonic individualism was in the main sternly repressed. The admirers of the medieval ages have indeed represented that period as one of wonderful organic unity; but that that unity was unstable and deceptive, and not a true synthesis of the discordant elements, is witnessed by continued conflicts throughout the Middle

Ages among the different traditions, and in the
final breakdown of medieval civilization, and
the rebirth of Paganism in the Renaissance.
The Renaissance was, indeed, in one aspect
simply the re-awaking of the traditions of
classic Greece and Rome to their full strength
in Western civilization, and it at once made
evident their conflict with the Hebrew-
Christian tradition.[34] From the Renaissance
period onward it has been difficult to say which
of the conflicting traditions in question has
been predominant. The modern world has
certainly had no better success in obtaining
a true synthesis of these conflicting traditions
than the medieval world. On the whole,
however, since the Renaissance, the traditions of Greek and Roman civilization have
been uppermost among European peoples.

To add still further confusion, modern
civilization has generated within itself certain
new forces which, though based upon the
traditions of ancient civilization, yet are very

far from being harmonious with them or even among themselves. Hence at the present time we witness not merely the conflict of the inconsistent traditions of four ancient cultures, but also the development of certain new movements within modern civilization itself, which have as yet far from reached their final development.

The first of these great modern movements is the rise of individualism and its obverse, the decline of authority. This movement, to be sure, was rooted in the Teutonic tradition of individual liberty, to which the Renaissance gave a rebirth. The earliest manifestation of this movement was seen in the Protestant Reformation, which must now be acknowledged to have been not so much a protest against ecclesiastical abuses as an expression of Teutonic individualism, and a revolt against ecclesiastical authority of any sort. The next great manifestation of rising individualism was in the Democratic movement, which had its earliest beginnings about the period of the Reformation, but which culminated in the nineteenth century by the establishment of popular governments among most European peoples.

Along with these emancipatory movements in Church and State, there gradually grew up an extreme individualistic view of life. An egoistic theory of human nature, which claimed that men never acted save from self-interest, and that enlightened self-interest was therefore the best guide of conduct, became an established tradition in Western civilization. The State and even the more spontaneous, natural social groups came to be regarded as forms of contract. The good of life, however, could consist only in the pleasure, or happiness, of individuals, for self-interest could aim at nothing else. The inevitable conclusion therefore was that institutions could and should be changed to suit the pleasure of individuals. Such extreme individualistic views necessarily proved revolutionary in a society honey-combed with ancient abuses, and in which all progressive reformation of the social order had been resisted for over three centuries; the result was the violent outbreak of the French Revolution.

The movement to emancipate the individual from all restrictions of authority has been supposed by some to have reached its culmination in the French Revolution; but it is now hardly necessary to point out that this movement has as yet far from spent its force. The tradition of individualism has continued to grow in Western civilization down to the present moment. Even our democracy has threatened to degenerate into mere *laissez-faire* individualism, and thus discredit itself, while individualism is now manifesting itself in new realms, such as the family, where its growth had scarcely been anticipated.[35]

Any limit of the individualistic movement, short of sheer anarchy, is indeed hard to discern on the present horizon of Western civilization. Our fathers rightly thought that

[35] On the decline of authority, see Ferrero, *Ancient Rome and Modern America*, p. 204.

the emancipation of the human spirit was one of the noblest causes to which men could devote themselves. They even thought that human history might be interpreted as such a progressive emancipation. They could scarcely have been expected to foresee that in the name of such "emancipation" individuals would demand to be released from a well-ordered and stable family life, that women would demand to be emancipated even from the natural burdens of motherhood, and that some men would demand to be freed from the restraints of any moral code whatsoever. While, therefore, historically the individualistic movement has conferred some of the greatest benefits upon Western civilization, and in many countries has still much beneficent work to do, yet it must be judged at the same time as perhaps the greatest menace of the present to social order, and so to civilization.

Partly owing to the freeing of the individual, partly owing to the re-discovery of the work of the Greeks, science also entered into a new life in the period of the Renaissance. The scientific movement, which then started, has been the second great force which has shaped modern civilization. One can scarcely, indeed, exaggerate the importance of this movement, even if regarded quite in its spiritual aspect; for it has so enlarged man's world, so broken up the foundations of old beliefs, that men have even forgotten that there is such a force as tradition in society. Moreover, it has given man such a mastery over physical nature that it has enlarged his hopes and expectations for the present life beyond even the dreams of the ancient world. This has been more especially true of the later developments of modern science; for after harnessing nature to man's use, it has boldly turned its attention to man's body and mind and has proclaimed that it can control these also. Finally, it has turned the searchlight of its criticism upon human institutions and social organization, and they also seem destined to pass under its sway.

Yet again, owing largely to the mistaken opposition of the Church to scientific research, science has tended to generate some socially negative traditions in Western civilization. It has tended to exclude the psychic or spiritual entirely from its domain, and to make all its interpretations in purely physical or mechanistic terms. Thus modern science has come often to take a negative attitude toward many of the higher social values, and this negative attitude has as a rule been most pronounced in those countries in which the teachers of religion have most opposed science.

Partly as a result of the emancipation of the individual from hampering restrictions, partly as a result of the development of scientific knowledge, a revolution took place in human industry in the latter part of the eighteenth and in the beginning of the nineteenth centuries.[36] The industry of the Middle

---

[36] For a good general survey of the industrial revolution, see Ely, *Evolution of Industrial Society*, especially Chapter III.

Ages had been carried on in households or in small shops where workmen belonging to the same guild worked together, owning very largely their tools and selling the products of their industry. Under such conditions the workman received practically all the product of his labour, and he was free, after accepting the law of the land and the requirements of his guild, to labour as he chose. But these primitive industrial conditions were changed as soon as machines took the place of hand labour toward the end of the eighteenth and in the beginning of the nineteenth centuries. Machines were relatively costly and could not be owned by independent labourers, but had to be owned by a wealthy class, the capitalist class.

Again, great factories came to replace small shops because it was economical to group machines and labourers together in one large plant. Thus the hand industry and guild industry of later medieval times came to be replaced by the machine industry and factory system of the present day. While there was great gain

to society at large in all this, through the great
increase of production of manufactured ar-
ticles, yet there was a considerable loss to the
labouring man. The labouring man lost especially his relative freedom and independence.
Owning no longer the tools with which he
worked and becoming specialized in his labour,
he seemed but little more than a cog in the
vast industrial machine. Hence the tendency
of capitalism has been to dehumanize the conditions under which the labouring man works.

Moreover, while capitalistic industry tended
to regard the individual labourer as simply a
machine, it tended also to make the individual
labourer himself, rather than his class or his
family, the unit in production. It minimized
the differences between the sexes and also
between children and adults. Industrial development thus powerfully reacted to promote
individualism still further, while on account
of its dehumanizing conditions it tended at
the same time to foster materialistic ideals of
life.

A further consequence of the industrial

revolution has been the enormous growth of wealth in the modern world. While this wealth has not been adequately shared by the labouring classes or even by the masses generally, a larger portion of human society has been emancipated from all fear of want than ever before in human history. In other words, the enormous wealth of modern times has stimulated luxury and self-indulgence in some classes of society almost beyond belief.[37] It has made it possible for many to escape from the consequences of conduct from which under more primitive social conditions they could not have escaped. The development of science, especially of the medical sciences, has also placed in the hands of our wealthy classes the means of defying to a certain extent physical and moral laws.

Finally, our industrial system has tended, for the reasons mentioned, to generate antagonism between economic classes. Class conflicts have been an increasingly disturbing

[37] On the increase of luxury in modern life, see Ferrero, *Ancient Rome and Modern America*, p. 208.

factor in our social order. Class interest has become too much a war-cry of contending factions. Worse still, a tradition of class hatred has been growing up within Western nations, sedulously fostered by some of the non-privileged, and often unwisely stimulated by the privileged. Thus a gulf, not only in actual conditions of life, but also in feeling, has been developing between the socially more fortunate and socially less fortunate—a gulf which the sympathy and understanding necessary for social solidarity finds it difficult to bridge. The tradition of the solidarity of class threatens to strangle the tradition of the solidarity of humanity.

Another movement which must be mentioned as having had a marked effect upon modern civilization is the so-called "critical movement" in modern thought, though it is scarcely to be distinguished from the extreme development of the doctrine of individualism, on the one hand, and of scientific thought, on the other. Now, public criticism is a part of the mechanism of social growth. It is, indeed, the very breath of life of those free societies in which change is rapid.[38] But criticism in order to be helpful must be constructive. It must pick out from the old situation and conserve whatever is of value in building up the new institution or order. But criticism, like all the instruments of the social life, is apt to go to an extreme, and become purely destructive and negative. Such a destructive criticism attacked in the nineteenth century practically all the institutions and values of society. Probably the chief impetus to such criticism were abuses in the existing social order, especially those upheld by the Church and the State. As an extreme reaction from these abuses, purely negative doctrines regarding many of the values connected with religion, morality, government, and the family, sprang up in the eighteenth and nineteenth centuries, and became widely diffused in certain classes. Hence the origin of that "social negativism"

[38] *Sociology in Its Psychological Aspects*, pp. 152–4; 334–8.

which we have already spoken of as the most
ominous and threatening thing on the present
horizon of Western civilization. For, while
criticism began with the noble work of freeing
man from superstition and exploitation, it has
ended in such absolute social negations as the
amoralism of Nietzsche and the exaltation of
violence by Syndicalism. Thus a tradition of
"moral anarchy" has gradually been established and tolerated in Western nations, a
condition which, if sanity and like-mindedness
play the part in maintaining social order usually ascribed to them by sociologists, must be
held responsible for much of the social disorder
of the present, and which may yet ultimately
prove destructive of all the higher values of
civilization.

On the other hand, in the later eighteenth
and through the whole of the nineteenth century, there took place a steady revival of humanitarianism, and the hopeful rise of many
humanitarian movements. This may reasonably be ascribed in large measure to a fuller

appreciation of the social implications of the ethics of the religion which had been nominally accepted by Western nations for over a millennium; but it was also in part due to the emancipation of the masses, to increasing knowledge of humanity, to scientific invention and discovery, and to the increasing economic inter-dependence of the world at large. The humanitarianism of the nineteenth century was, to be sure, often superficial, inconsistent, fitful, and purely emotional; but it freed the slave, emancipated woman, educated the masses, organized public and private philanthropy, tried to suppress the liquor traffic, to carry a knowledge of Christianity to the heathen world, and even to put an end to war between nations. Other movements of the nineteenth century which we have mentioned must be regarded as having limits and perhaps necessarily both good and bad sides. But the humanitarian movement, if it can be purged of its weaknesses and allied with humanistic science, alone promises the unlimited, peaceful, all-round development of humanity in the future. It was the most precious tradition which the nineteenth century bequeathed to the twentieth.

On account of all these factors and many minor ones, the nineteenth century was a century of great social change and unrest. While it was the most progressive century in recorded human history, yet it failed on the whole to develop a constructive social programme. If any ideals dominated it, they were the ideals of individual liberty and material achievement. But these ideals, we are now beginning to see, are almost wholly negative in their implications for the higher social life of man. When taken as ends in themselves, they tend to degenerate into that individualism and materialism which threaten the very stability of Western civilization itself.

It should be unnecessary to add that the peculiar features of modern civilization have been greatly exaggerated in the social life of the American people. Upon the virgin soil

of the New World the seeds of modern individualism and industrialism and of social
negativism have sprung up into gigantic
growths. All this has been accentuated rather
than lessened by the influx into the United
States of millions of immigrants from all
lands. The social confusion which characterizes modern civilization generally, has been
greatly increased in America through the attempt to mix peoples of many different traditions and discordant ideals of life. That like-
mindedness, which is most important for social
peace and solidarity, is especially absent from
American society as a whole. Never before,
says Professor Giddings, has any nation at-
tempted to "mingle in one political aggregate,
first, antagonistic races, and secondly, the
most miscellaneous assortment of nationalities,
standards of living, religious, moral and political traditions, temperaments and opinions,
ever nominally combined as a single people."

And yet it is perhaps this very intermingling
of different races, religions, and traditions of
all sorts, which has given rise in America more

than elsewhere to the sentiment of a common humanity, and which perhaps fits it best to lead the humanitarian movement. What will come out of this "melting pot of the nations" no one can yet foresee. Optimistic sociologists are fond of asserting that out of the contact and intermingling of cultures a higher culture is bound to result through the survival of what is best in each. But blind optimism is no more warranted here than elsewhere; for careful scientific study shows that people are quite as apt to imitate the worst in each other, as the best; and that the constant selection of the best results only from high intelligence and character directed by wise leadership.

Another influence which has specifically affected American society, as has often been pointed out by historians, is the tradition of frontier life. On the frontier, civilization is often to a certain extent left behind. Not infrequently the rule of force is the only recognized law, and a stark individualism dominates practical life. The social values associated with a well-ordered social life are given a low estimate or even tend to be forgotten. Now, practically every American community in its early beginnings represented the frontier; and long after the frontier stage of development was passed the traditions of the frontier have survived in American communities. This is shown by the statistics of divorce, homicide, and lynching, as well as by the traditions of initiative, individual energy, and self-dependence in the American population. Moreover, the frontier frequently afforded great opportunities for the individual to enrich himself through speculation, the exploitation of natural resources, or similar practices. Thus the traditions of commercialism and of a predatory, individualistic business ethics, originally from European motherlands, became fastened on the majority of the American people also.

Such, in briefest outline, are the chief historical and traditional elements which enter into the social problem of the present. And let us always remember that the geographical, biological, and spiritual elements in that problem act only in their historic settings. The traditions of four ancient and conflicting cultures have mingled in our own; while recent history has developed many and often antagonistic forces in our civilization. We have thus far failed to make a true organic synthesis of these; and it is no wonder that confusion and conflict as to ideals of life have resulted. But this is no reason for supposing the social problem insoluble, though it may take the labour and wisdom of many generations to build the ideal society of humanity.

The exact synthesis which we should seek of these historical elements in the reconstruction of our civilization will become clear in later chapters. But it already is evident that in building for the future we must decide in particular, whether we will follow more largely the leadership of Rome or the leadership of Judea.

Eugenics.

CHAPTER III

PHYSICAL AND BIOLOGICAL ELEMENTS IN THE SOCIAL PROBLEM

THERE is no escaping the fact that human societies exist under certain fixed physical conditions which make them possible. Society may be a spiritual fact; but, so far as we know, it is possible only within very narrow range of physical conditions. Even a small fluctuation in temperature, for instance, would wipe out human life on this planet; while a still smaller change in climate would put an end to all higher civilization. Man's boasted mastery over nature is seen to be a very feeble thing in the face of the earthquake, the tornado, the flood, or even in the face of the physiological laws of his own body, or forces like natural selection operating in the organic world. Man can exist only by submission to such forces; he can progress only as he understands them and acts in harmony with them.

Now, these familiar facts have led to attempts to interpret all human life, even civilization itself, in physical terms. Because some sets of physical conditions are absolutely necessary to man's well-being, it is argued that they alone, or in conjunction with other physical conditions, entirely determine his social life. Now, it is no longer necessary to refute "geographical determinism," for serious students of human society. It is seen to be like saying that because the shining of the sun is absolutely necessary for man's existence, therefore the sun absolutely determines the life of man. The conditions and the determining factors of social life have been confused. On the other hand, the interpretation of human society in terms of a purely biological "struggle for existence" is not quite so dead, but it rests in last analysis upon no sounder basis. The physical struggle for existence is a very real fact in human experience, and the resulting "natural selection" a very great factor in social evolution; but there is no reason for supposing it the only factor in that process. Rather, as we have seen, the process of social and cultural development is very different from the process of organic development, even though the latter itself may turn out to be something more than purely physical.

In recognizing the very great part played by physical and biological elements in the social problem, we wish expressly to repudiate, as unscientific, physical and purely biological theories of human society, and to warn the reader against that one-sidedness in social theory and practice which results from too exclusive attention to these physical elements. Nevertheless, because human life develops, as it were, about two poles, one physical and the other psychic, we must in our study of the social problem give due credit to the physical. It is manifest that the heritage of civilization consists, not merely of spiritual elements, but also (1) of a favourable physical environment with suitable natural resources for the development of the economic and technologic life; (2) of the individual health and bodily vigour of the whole population; (3) of a sound racial heredity, or germ plasm, which shall transmit from generation to generation the potential qualities of body and mind in individuals necessary to meet the exacting demands of an increasingly complex civilization. Even if natural resources, health, and heredity can be controlled only by education and government, they are objective facts which must be put foremost in any scientific discussion of social reconstruction.

Man's control over climatic and general meteorologic conditions is still very limited, but his control over natural resources in the soil, in water, in fauna and flora, and in minerals can be very great. The movement for the conservation of natural resources has happily gained such headway in most civilized nations that it is only necessary to say that it rests upon the soundest ethical and scientific basis. Man has been such a ruthless plunderer of the riches of mother nature that he has in places left her destitute. Instead of conserving and developing the gifts of the earth, he has exploited them too often for his own individual benefit. Instead of tilling the soil, he has often "mined" it, as it were, to get selfishly for himself and his own whatever wealth he could wring from it, impoverishing future generations. He has cut down forests which he never grew, without planting any in their place, sometimes rendering thereby whole districts uninhabitable. He has wantonly destroyed whole species of animals which might have been of possible use to future generations. He has needlessly robbed the earth of its mineral resources in order to enrich himself more rapidly, though the civilization of the future may depend upon these. All this is, of course, a result of our predatory civilization; and the fatal weakness of the conservation movement is that it demands a consideration of humanity itself, the humanity which is to be as well as that which now is,—such as has not yet established itself among our supreme social values. In other words, it demands for its success a humanity-wide altruism, uncorrupted by any mere self-interest. But that such a movement has made some headway is one of the most encouraging signs in Western civilization; and we must recognize that the sciences connected with it, such as the New Agriculture, must have part in the solution of the social problem. In this connection, in order to show the wide bearings of the agricultural problem upon the social problem generally, it may be well to cite the words of one of the profounder critics of American civilization: [39] "The country side has in the last half century been too much neglected, exactly as began to be the case in the Roman Empire at the beginning of the second century. It is easy to guess what must be the consequence of this lop-sided arrangement. The cities grow bigger; industries increase in size; the luxury and the needs of the masses, crowded together in the cities, augment. On the other hand, there is no propor-

[39] See Ferrero, *Ancieni Rome and Modern America,* p. 86.

tionate increase in the productiveness of the land. And so the increase in wealth is accompanied by an increasing *scarcity* of the fruits of the earth."

Of even greater importance than the conservation of natural resources is the conservation and development of physical health in the population. As Herbert Spencer said, *"To be a good animal is the first requisite to success in life, and to be a nation of good animals is the first condition of national prosperity."* But through the slums of our cities, through unsanitary work and workshops, through starvation wages and long hours, through alcoholism and sexual vice, through luxurious habits of living and social strain, Western civilization has been seriously undermining health instead of building it up. As an eminent American physician has said:

"The progressive civilization of the last hundred years has worked terribly against the health and perpetuity of the whole race. This is seen in the reduced vitality of the multitude that inhabit closely built cities, in the diminished size of families, in the incapacity of many women to bear and nurse children, in the disproportionate increase of the insane, defectives and criminally inclined. Such cities as London, Paris, Berlin, New York, and Chicago bear witness that modern civilization is all the time preparing and promoting its own destruction."

With such a statement every careful student of social conditions must heartily agree, except that one may doubt the propriety of calling a civilization progressive which has done such things. From this standpoint the whole public health movement looms up with a new importance. The rôle of sanitary science and public hygiene is seen to be a social one, which affects the whole life of humanity, both now and in the future. It is not merely a question of the sympathetic relief or prevention of the sufferings of a few scattered individuals; it is rather a question of controlling the physical factor in living together, and of conserving the physical basis of civilization. We must put a stop to the destruction of individual health in mine and factory, in our cities and in our unsanitary rural regions, both by work and by vicious habits, if we are to have either a satisfactory social life in the present or continued progress in the future.

In fact, every preventable disease, every condition which needlessly undermines the vitality of a population is a direct menace and obstacle to all that makes for higher civilization. The sacrifice of life through industrial accidents and diseases, through overwork and underpay, through unsanitary dwellings, through commercialized pandering to men's vicious appetites, we must cease to tolerate among us if we are to progress either morally or physically. The evils of war are great, but they are no greater than these evils of peace which we have tolerated too long. Professor Irving Fisher has shown that the annual loss to the United States alone through preventable diseases and deaths is over $1,500,000,000.[40]

[40] See his report on *National Vitality, its Wastes and Conservation*, Senate Document No. 676, pp. 634, 741.

The economic loss is, however, only a small part of the real loss through the existence of preventable diseases. There is also the intellectual and moral loss of the removal from society, either temporarily through ill-health, or permanently through death, of individuals performing every function in the family, the community, and the nation. We cannot safely assume that preventable disease and death remove chiefly the unfit in society. On the contrary, under present social conditions at least, the victims are perhaps as frequently the capable and efficient as the incapable and inefficient. In any case, one of the prime conditions of normal social life is that there be a prolonged working period for both men and women. If there is some advantage in a progressive society in having a preponderance in it of youth, there is also infinite social loss in having individuals cut off just as they are prepared to render the largest social service. All arrangements in the family, the community and the nation suffer because of the needless uncertainty of life and health. There can be no solution of the social problem until the problems of health are brought under social control.

Fortunately all the movements that can be included under public health and preventive medicine—the anti-tuberculosis movement, the housing movement, infant welfare, industrial hygiene, school hygiene, urban and rural sanitation—are well under way among civilized nations, even though much remains to be done. Only the movements against alcoholism and sexual vice lack popular support in some communities. The trouble with all these movements is that they too often lack the social point of view. Their leaders do not always see that all social problems hang together, and that they are merely dealing with *the* social problem in some of its physical aspects. Tuberculosis as a preventable disease, e. g., is rooted in all sorts of physical and moral conditions in society. One cannot touch the tuberculosis problem without picking up with it the problems of human industry, morality, heredity—in fact the whole problem of human living together, the social problem. There is urgent need for a "medical sociology" which shall see the inter-relations of these physical problems with the spiritual aspects of human life.

But the social problem cannot be solved until we can control in some degree that physical relation between generations which we term heredity. Next after tradition, heredity is, perhaps, the most important constitutive element of human society, because it gives continuity to the social life on the physical side. If it is important that we conserve in every reasonable way the life and health of the individual, it is even more important, in any long view of human life, that we conserve the integrity of the hereditary elements which produce each new generation. For the stream of life may be polluted in two ways, either at its source or along its banks. Disease, alcoholism, vice, and unsanitary surroundings may pollute the stream of life after its start, but when we allow the biologically unfit to become parents we pollute it at its source; and this is in the long run the more serious, for life polluted at its source never can cleanse itself. It is the manifest duty of humanitarian ethics, therefore, to insist that every child born into the world shall have a right start in life—a good birth. Now, this means that it shall have a sound heredity.[41] We need not lose our interest in the influences of the environment which shape character because we are interested in every child having a right physical heredity. On the contrary, if we are interested in every child having a right start in life physically, we should be all the more interested in keeping favourable the forces in the environment which may affect character or even destroy health and life. Otherwise, from a social life point of view, our work is in vain. *Recognition of the importance of heredity, then, is perfectly compatible with the recognition of the importance of nurture or environment.* However much faith we may have

---

[41] Cf. Saleeby, *Parenthood and Race Culture;* also *Methods of Race Regeneration.*

that in the spiritual elements of life lies the key to the control of individual character and social development, yet we must recognize the physical elements as the basis of our social life; and among these physical elements heredity is easily of the first practical importance.

What, then, is heredity? And how can it be controlled? Without going into technicalities, let us consider the first question.[42]

We all understand what heredity is in a general way. We plant seed in the ground, and from it expect a plant of a certain type to be produced. We know that as much depends upon the seed as upon the soil, moisture, temperature, and light, the factors in the environment. We do not expect a superior type

[42] The substance of the remainder of this Chapter was delivered as a lecture before the University of Missouri in April, 1913, under the patronage of Mrs. Huntington Wilson, and was later published by her in a book entitled: *Eugenics, Twelve University Lectures* (Dodd, Mead and Co., 1914).

Cf. Davenport, *Heredity in Relation to Eugenics;* also, Guyer, *Being Well-Born.*

of cabbage, say, to grow from an inferior kind of seed; neither do we expect the cabbage to grow without the proper conditions of soil, moisture, temperature, and cultivation. Now the seed stands for the hereditary elements involved in such a situation. The heredity, in other words, is *what is given in the germ,* and it is manifest that no attention to environment can possibly develop anything but the potentialities of the germ. Now, the case with human beings is not different from what it is with plants. As in the plant world, so in the human world, heredity is alone creative of individual qualities. The environment can only modify those qualities, though we must not fail to remember that, so far as social conduct is concerned, man is probably the most modifiable of all living forms.[43] Now, if heredity is what is given in the germ, it is evident that *nothing can be inherited except the traits which are inherent in the germ cells.* These cells, out of which the new individual arises, modern biology teaches, are a separate

[43] See Thomson's *Heredity,* pp. 242–9.

series of cells distinct from and more or less independent of the body cells. Hence, the impossibility of parents transmitting to offspring traits which they have acquired during their lifetime, for there is no way by which specific modifications in the cells of the body can possibly reproduce themselves in the germ cells. This fact of the non-transmissibility of acquired traits is known as Weismann's law of the non-inheritance of acquired characters. Though there has been much debate of this law, rightly understood it seems self-evident, when we remember that the germ cells are separate and distinct from the body cells. Under such circumstances it is impossible to conceive that a bodily mutilation could be transmitted from parent to offspring; likewise, that a functionally-produced modification in the body of the parent organism could be transmitted. A clear grasp, therefore, of the truth that nothing is inherited except the characteristics of the family stock, the traits which are inherent in the germ plasm itself, will save many questions.

Weismann's law is, however, often misunderstood by people generally to be the doctrine that the life of the parent organism in no way affects the life of the offspring; that no matter what the individual parent does, it will not affect his offspring. This is, of course, a gross misunderstanding of Weismann's doctrine. Weismann knew, as well as anyone, that the germ cells receive their nutrition from the blood, and hence may possibly be influenced in many ways by the character of that nutrition. As yet, however, scientific evidence is lacking as to the amount and character of the influence upon the germ plasm through nutrition. The evidence seems to point mainly in a negative direction, that is, that the germ cells may be influenced by poisons and by malnutrition, but probably not in the opposite direction. Thus, the evidence seems to be fairly sufficient to warrant the conclusion that a large amount of alcohol in the blood, sufficient to poison the whole system, will poison the germ cells and set up degenerative changes in them. The offspring of confirmed alcoholics are, therefore, apt to be under-vitalized or afflicted with various forms of degeneracy, such as feeble-mindedness, epilepsy, and insanity. This is, at least, the most conservative, scientific view at the present, though it is still much debated. It will be noted, however, that in this case there has been no inheritance of any specific acquired traits. The poison of alcohol has simply set up degenerative changes which affect the germ cells themselves. It is highly probable that the toxins elaborated by certain diseases may produce similar results; certain statistics, at any rate, seem to indicate that to parents in the advanced stages of such a disease as tuberculosis normal children are seldom born. As an example of the effect of malnutrition on the germ cells, it is only necessary to point out that the malnutrition which accompanies advanced age, shows itself especially clearly in this connection. According to Dr. Bertillon of Paris, who has made elaborate investigations along this line, fathers above the age of sixty years rarely beget perfectly healthy children. Much investigation is, however, still necessary before we can fully decide how far the life history of the parent organism may influence biologically, that is, by heredity, the life of the offspring. It is certain, however, that we are not warranted in assuming that no matter how we live our life will not affect the physical constitution and health of our children. Rather the only safe conclusion for the present is that we should live on the highest physical plane, not only for the sake of our own efficiency, but also for the sake of our descendants.

Another fact which should always be remembered in connection with heredity is that inheritance is equal from both parents, but traits are seemingly transmitted as units. This fact gives rise to what is known as Mendel's law, according to which there is no permanent blending of different traits in a series of generations, but on the contrary contrasted traits tend to segregate in definite and regular proportions after the first filial generation. For example, if feeble-minded persons intermarry with normal persons, their children in the first generation will be apparently all normal persons.[44] But if these children of feeble-minded and normal persons intermarry among themselves, their offspring will be found to be one-fourth feeble-minded and three-fourths apparently normal persons. But if these latter intermarry it is found that two-thirds of them will again have offspring in the proportion one-fourth feeble-minded and three-fourths apparently normal, while only one-third will have wholly normal offspring. This shows that in the second generation one-fourth were pure normals, one-fourth feeble-minded, and one-half hybrids which appeared normal, but which were in fact not so, so far as their germ cells were concerned.

Mendel's law thus shows us the manner of transmission of hereditary traits in individual cases. It is a highly important law for eu-

[44] Assuming, of course, that feeble-mindedness behaves like a simple recessive unit character. But see Goddard, *The Kallikak Family;* also, *Feeblemindedness: Its Causes and Consequences* (1914).

genics, especially because it shows us the results of the crossing of normal with abnormal stocks. It will be noted that, according to Mendel's law, no secure knowledge of heredity can be gained from the observance of just two consecutive generations, but only through the study of three or more generations. In human society, on account of the crossing of numerous stocks, or bio-types, as they are called, practically every mating results in hybrid offspring. Hence the full result of such mating may not be seen until the second, third, or even fourth filial generation.[45]

One further fact should be mentioned in connection with the modern doctrine of heredity, and that is, that apparently minute variations or "fluctuations," as they are termed by biologists, are probably not inherited. Only the larger variations, variations in quality, not in degree, are clearly transmissible. Minute personal traits of the in-

[45] For a clear discussion of Mendelism as well as the whole modern theory of heredity, in addition to the references above, see Walter, *Genetics*.

dividual, in other words, though they may do much to make personality, are not transmissible, but, as we have said, only the characteristics of the family stock, the traits which are inherent in the germ plasm.[46] These hereditary traits, however, affect every quality of the individual, not only his bodily make-up, but, also, in a lesser degree, his mental and moral character.

Now, the science which aims at the practical control of human heredity is called Eugenics, which Sir Francis Galton, its founder, defined as "the science which deals with all influences that improve the inborn qualities of a race." At first sight it might seem that this science was simply the application to the human species of the biological laws which we have just discussed, and that it had nothing to do with sociology. But on further thought we see that the application of our knowledge of heredity in human society involves col-

[46] This, at least, is the conclusion of Johannsen, the Danish biologist, from his experiments.

lective control over the whole reproductive process. As Galton himself said, eugenics must be "the study of agencies *under social control* which may improve or impair the racial qualities of future generations, either physically or mentally." It must be included, therefore, as Mr. Victor Branford contends,[47] within the scope of sociology, at least of any sociology which applies itself to the solution of the social problem.

For it is evident that eugenics can do nothing to improve the human breed without controlling the institution of marriage and sex relations generally in society. Practically, therefore, the problem of eugenics in the present order of society is simply the problem of securing wise marriages—wise, that is, from the biological standpoint. The problem of eugenics is, then, a sociological problem, which, however, demands expert biological knowledge for its solution.

There is much to commend and at the same time many dangers and difficulties in the

[47] *Interpretations and Forecasts*, pp. 3, 403.

present eugenics movement. The chief danger is to be found in the over-emphasis of the importance of heredity, and of the biological element generally, in human society. If it has been a common mistake of social thinkers in the past to underrate the importance of this element, it may easily happen that in the future too great emphasis may be laid upon it. Human society, as we have seen, is primarily a psychic or spiritual matter, and social or cultural evolution is only based on and conditioned by organic evolution. Social improvement is by no means mere biological improvement.[48] It follows that an exclusively biological view of human society is one of those dangerous one-sided doctrines which prove negative toward other aspects of our social life. There is as little excuse now for theorizing about an abstract biologic man in society as for theorizing about an abstract economic man. Every sane student of society knows that neither exists. It is inexcusable,

[48] *Cf.* Hobhouse, *Social Evolution and Political Theory*, Chapter III.

therefore, for the eugenist to ally himself practically with the materialist by overlooking the spiritual factors in our social life.

Even if we regard man from a purely physical standpoint, there are beside the hereditary or inborn traits of individuals their acquired traits or habits. Now, there is no sufficient evidence to show that the inborn traits of individuals determine in any great degree their acquired traits, especially in the realm of conduct. On the contrary, these latter seem to be more largely determined by the social environment, especially the "subjective environment" of ideas, ideals, and values which constitute the tradition of the social group of which he is a member. The inborn traits of our forefathers three thousand years back probably did not differ appreciably from our own; but they were savages or barbarians, and we are civilized. Apparently, in the normal man, habits of many varied sorts may be built upon the basis of his inborn traits; yet the former are vastly more important from a social and moral standpoint;

for inborn traits, so far as we know, neither adjust the individual to civilization nor produce high moral character.

The eugenist cannot be pardoned, therefore, when he forgets that we all are born savages; that civilization and most of its virtues are acquired traits; and that, therefore, the problems of our civilization are essentially spiritual. Yet he is right when he insists that certain qualities and capacities of the hereditary elements of the germ plasm, must furnish the basis upon which all human civilization and all acquired mental and moral characters of the individual must be built. We have only to look at the feeble-minded in order to see this. He is right, therefore, when he emphasizes the inadequacy of all social reform which leaves heredity out of account. On the other hand, a sanely developed eugenics movement will recognize the inadequacy of all attempts at social reform through paying attention to heredity alone. It will make no claim that it is any more than one of many agencies which may be employed for the improvement of human social life. But since heredity is the basis of individual character, it must be controlled if we are to control adequately the development of character; and as individual character, physical, intellectual and moral, is the ultimate problem in human society, we must learn to control heredity in order to solve the social problem.[49]

But there are great practical difficulties in the way of the success of the eugenics movement, even greater than the theoretical dangers just pointed out. The individualism developed by modern civilization has shown itself especially in sex relations. Marriage has been based solely upon romantic affection and its primary purpose is supposed to be the happiness of the parties concerned. To control marriage and sex relations in the interest of society is a difficult matter; yet, as we have said, this is the real problem involved in a

[49] Anyone interested in the problem of heredity in human society should read Dr. H. H. Goddard's illuminating work on *The Kallikak Family.*

rational eugenics programme. It would be a great mistake to assert at the beginning that this could not be done. As Sir Francis Galton pointed out, the institution of marriage has been subjected among practically all peoples, to numerous regulations, some of them of the most absurd character. If this is true, then it must be evident that there is no insuperable difficulty in the way of the control of marriage in the interests of a stronger and better race. The method of control in such a civilization as ours would, however, manifestly have to be different from methods often used in the past. It could not be through superstition, nor even mainly through legal coercion. It would have to be mainly through the power of education, ideals, and public opinion. A practical eugenics programme, therefore, must direct itself to influencing these three great agencies of social control.

Another difficulty of a eugenics programme in modern society is the confusion regarding ideals of life, which we have already pointed out as so marked a trait in our civilization, and the consequent disagreement as to what are desirable qualities in the individual. It would seem, however, as has often been remarked, that even *we* might agree as to the desirability of health, energy, intelligence, and self-control in individuals as contrasted with their extreme opposites.

A temporary limitation of any eugenics programme at present is, of course, the imperfectness of our knowledge of human heredity. But this is being remedied yearly, and exact biological knowledge seems probable even within the near future.

As to the need of a eugenics programme in modern society, there is practically no difference of opinion among careful students. Long before Galton formulated his programme, sociologists and social workers had often pointed out the need of it. It has long been evident that the greater or less degree of cessation of natural selection brought about in certain social classes by wealth, unwise charity, and other means, has resulted in the gradual production of an enormous number of hereditary defectives, among practically all civilized people. If we take the United States as an example, there are in its hundred million of population over one-half million mental defectives alone, including in that term only the manifestly feeble-minded, the chronic insane, and the epileptic. Recent investigations, moreover, show that a very large proportion of the criminal, pauper, and vicious classes must also be included in the mentally defective classes. In a large majority of these cases, heredity is responsible for their condition. If we add to these mental defectives all those who suffer from serious physical defects, the total number of defective stock in the United States cannot fall much short of three million persons. Of this number, something over one-half million are cared for in institutions, placing upon the normal population a burden of probably about a thousand million dollars annually. When we consider that the defective persons outside of institutions are also frequently a burden upon the normal population, we can see the immense financial burden which our defective stock imposes upon our nation, to say nothing of the enormous total burden which must rest upon the whole family of civilized nations by reason of the existence of a large per cent of defective individuals in their population. Moreover, when we reflect that a very large per cent of these defectives are married and become parents, and that the lower types of defectives, especially the feeble-minded, have a much higher birth rate than the normal population, we can readily see that the peril of diffusing throughout our general population the traits of these defective strains is not exaggerated by eugenists.

On the other hand, investigation shows that in nearly all Western nations the educated and socially fortunate classes fail to reproduce even sufficiently to keep up their numbers, and that this tendency is rapidly increasing. Thus in England, according to Whetham,[50] the birth rate of aristocratic families declined from over seven children per each fertile

[50] *The Family and the Nation*, p. 139.

marriage in the decade preceding 1840 to 3.13 children per each fertile marriage in the decade ending 1890. Meanwhile the percentage of fertile marriages among the aristocracy had greatly decreased. In Massachusetts in 1910 the native white stock showed a birth rate of only 14.8 per thousand annually of their population, while their death rate was 16.3.[51] On the other hand, the foreign born in Massachusetts in 1910 had a birth rate of 49.5 per thousand of their population, while their death rate was 15.5.[52] These figures seem to indicate that the socially more capable classes frequently fail to reproduce adequately, while other evidence, as we have already said, undoubtedly shows that the socially unfit reproduce more rapidly than the normal. Thus Western civilization is tolerating a

[51] It is scarcely necessary to point out that this stock represents largely the older families in Massachusetts, the stock which produced the great men of New England of the middle nineteenth century.

[52] See the whole discussion of this question of the decline of the birth rate in the writer's work on *Sociology and Modern Social Problems*, revised edition, 1913.

"reversal of selection," and such reversal of selection has been an important factor in the collapse of previous civilizations.

War also, whether civil or international, as has often been pointed out, is one of the agencies in human society under modern conditions which does most to promote a "reversal of selection." War not only prevents the normal reproduction of many of the strongest and fittest by removing them from family life, but it absolutely eliminates them. Nations can easily destroy their strongest and most capable elements by excessive militarism. But, on the other hand, as we have already shown, peace in itself is no guarantee that this "reversal of selection" shall cease. On the contrary, peace with unwise social arrangements and false ideals of living may be as noneugenic as war itself.

What, then, can be done? As soon as we turn to this practical question, the dangers and difficulties which confront a eugenics programme become again manifest. Especially is there danger of premature legislation forbidding marriage to certain classes of defectives. People are particularly prone to forget what the law can do and what it cannot do. There is no reason to suppose that the mere forbidding of legal marriage to certain classes of defectives will prevent their propagation in society, because it is probable that many of these defective individuals will find means of reproducing their kind outside of the marriage bond. Unwise laws, in other words, may not prevent the reproduction of the unfit, but only add to the burden of defectiveness the further burden of illegitimacy.

It may be worth our while to pause for a moment to see what the law can do in specific cases, and what it cannot do. It is in general a safe principle to lay down that society should not forbid marriage to any class of persons unless it is prepared to care for that class in institutions segregated from free social life, or, unless it is confident that public conscience and public opinion will be strong enough in its influence over that particular class to prevent even secret infractions of the law.

We often hear it said that legal marriage should be forbidden to the insane, the epileptic, and the feeble-minded. This is, of course, a correct theoretical position, but such a law would do little good unless it were backed up by provisions to care for and segregate these classes in institutions. The same remark, of course, applies to criminals and vicious persons; it would do little good to prohibit marriage to these unless provision for their segregation were made. We hear much now-a-days also, of laws to prohibit marriage unless both parties can present a physician's certificate showing reasonable soundness in body and mind. But, again it must be said that the State is not prepared to enforce such a law as yet, because in present society many of the persons who need theoretically such control would be practically least amenable to any form of legal control. On the other hand, while the State is not prepared to enforce such a law as yet, on account of the low condition of public morals, the Church, which is supposed to set the standard in ethical conduct, might very well require of all who come before it and ask for the sanction of religion upon their union, that they present some evidence to show reasonable soundness in body and mind. For how can the Church, the institution which stands for ideals in society, give its sanction to a marriage which, according to humanitarian doctrine, is essentially unethical? As a matter of fact, some churches in the United States have already established such regulations for the marriages solemnized by them, and such regulations seem to work well.

It must not be supposed from what has been said that eugenic regulation of marriage by law is impossible. All that has been said merely implies that legal regulation of marriage, for the more defective classes, must be backed up by adequate institutional and other social provisions. Eugenic regulation of marriage for the normal population by law is, of course, entirely possible where there is adequate backing of such laws by public opinion.

As examples of such laws, we might instance the laws forbidding marriage between first cousins and other near relatives. Careful investigation seems to show that the warrant for such laws, from a eugenic or biological standpoint, is ample. On account of the fact that many families have slight hereditary defects, cousin marriages multiply the chances of these defects being perpetuated, and even intensified. Hence, statistics show that cousin marriages result in the production of a very much larger percentage of defectives than marriages between persons more distantly related.

Other laws of a eugenic character, of course, are possible of enforcement, provided public opinion sufficiently sanctions them. Such a law, for example, would be a wise law restricting the class of immigrants admitted to any country. While it may be very difficult to determine by law, for the people who are already in any country, who shall be permitted to be parents of its future citizens, it ought not to be particularly difficult to act upon this principle with regard to the admission of our foreign immigrants. While the United States, e. g., have immigration laws already which exclude certain dependent and defective classes, in the opinion of experts these laws are still relatively ineffective and insufficient. An adequate selection could be made at comparatively small expense among our immigrants to exclude hereditary defectives by sending trained field workers to the countries from which they come.

Another legal measure, widely advocated at the present time in the name of eugenics, is the sterilization of habitual criminals and defectives. Eight or ten American states have already passed laws to provide for this, though few have had the courage to put such a law into operation. The general opinion of those who have made the most careful study of this measure is that it is a dangerous or, at least, a questionable law. The sterilization of criminals and defectives does very little to solve the real problems which those classes occasion in society. On the contrary, such a measure may intensify other evils. Thus, the sterilization of a feeble-minded woman leaving her at liberty in society, would in no way remove the menace which she is to the community, save it would prevent her becoming the mother of children. The unwisdom of such a half-way measure as this must, therefore, be manifest. Of course, there is no objection to the programme of the sterilization of markedly defective persons if it is accompanied by their segregation in institutions; but in such a case sterilization becomes unnecessary.

We come, therefore, to the permanent segregation in institutions of the more hopeless types of defectives as the only policy which society can afford to endorse in its war against racial deterioration. The usual objection to this policy, which has been advocated for over a generation by enlightened social workers, is that it is too expensive; that it would imply an enormous multiplication of institutions. The reply is that, while the immediate expense of such a programme of institutional development for defectives might be great, yet it would be a saving to society in the long run, an enormous saving if the principles of eugenics are true. Again, the expense is often exaggerated. Society has already undertaken the permanent segregation of one of these classes, namely, the insane, without any very great expense. The segregation of the feeble-minded would entail, if anything, less expense because many of these individuals can be made largely to support themselves in properly managed institutions of the farm colony type. It is estimated that there are, at least, 200,000 feeble-minded persons in the United States, a large percentage of whom should be cared for in institutions. As yet, however, only five states require feeble-minded persons to be committed to institutions just as the insane are committed by public authorities. Provisions for the chronic epileptic class, a very dangerous defective class, are even more deficient.

It may be remarked that wherever the

policy of segregation has been tried it has proved effective. Thus, in northern Italy in the province of Aosta, there existed for centuries a class of hereditary defectives known as *cretins*. These *cretins* suffered from a peculiar form of idiocy or imbecility associated with the degeneration of the thyroid gland which was hereditary. For a time, owing to their marriage being encouraged by the Church, their numbers greatly increased. In 1890, however, a policy of segregation was adopted, and by 1910 only a single *cretin* and three demi-*cretins* were left where hundreds had existed before. Modern society, therefore, cannot enter too soon upon this policy of segregation of pronounced defectives. There can be no question, moreover, as to the humanitarian grounds for such a policy, because it has been demonstrated that such defective persons are nearly always happier and better cared for in institutions than they would be outside, and they do not entail future generations with the burden of their defects.

Such is the extent to which the law can go wisely in aiding the eugenics movement. What law cannot accomplish, however, can be accomplished oftentimes by public opinion and public sentiment. Thus, it might be unwise, for example, at the present, either to forbid marriage to or provide for the segregation of certain classes in our population suffering merely from hereditary physical defects. But because these persons are normal mentally we might expect through the pressure of public opinion to bring them to forego marriage and parenthood. Such a class, for example, is the class of congenital or hereditary deaf-mutes. This is a defect which is highly transmissible if persons of this class intermarry. On the other hand, many congenital deaf-mutes are highly intelligent persons. It would seem desirable, neither to segregate this class nor to forbid them legal marriage, but to develop in them, through education and the pressure of public opinion, a eugenic conscience which, under ordinary circumstances, would probably lead the person suffering from such a defect not to marry.

Here, of course, questions may be raised which it is impossible as yet to answer with definiteness. Most hereditary defects behave, as the biologists would say, as recessive characters, that is, they do not appear in the first generation of children when persons having such defects intermarry with the normal population. Hence, it has been said by some eugenists that if defective persons would continually marry outside their defective class, these defects would gradually disappear from the germ plasm, and there would be, therefore, no eugenic objection to such marriages. But the danger of such a doctrine is obvious. There are so many defective stocks in existing society that the chances would be great that some of the children of the first generation who appeared normal might intermarry with a stock having a similar defect, then the defect would reappear in individuals. In this way defectiveness would be scattered in society rather than

eliminated. The safe counsel would, therefore, appear to be that persons having themselves marked physical or mental defects
should forego marriage altogether, while persons who come from family stocks in which
it is known such defects exist, should be careful to intermarry only with normal persons.
In this case there would be no danger of the
defect reappearing in later generations.

Since much work still remains to be done in
the scientific investigation of human heredity,
no hard and fast rules can be made for such
cases as we have just discussed. For the
present, therefore, the safe policy would seem
to be to leave such matters to enlightened
individual conscience to decide.

Such, then, is the negative programme of
eugenics. It would be a great mistake, however, to think of the eugenics movement as
entirely, or even chiefly, negative, aiming
simply at the elimination of hereditary defects in human stocks.[53] On the contrary, the

[53] One must not forget the problem of quantity as

founder of the eugenics movement, Sir Francis
Galton, himself considered the movement to
be primarily positive, aiming at the encouragement of marriage and parenthood among
the classes of superior endowments. In his
own language "The aim of eugenics is to
bring as many influences as can be reasonably
employed, to cause the useful classes in the
community to contribute *more* than their
proportion to the next generation." As we
have seen at the present time the birth rate
has fallen greatly among the socially more
fortunate classes, those best fitted to meet

well as quality in a population. Says Ferrero: "One of
the reasons why all the most ancient civilizations have
perished is that at the moment of their greatest glory
the population suddenly began to dwindle; and this
sterility which killed them was the effect to a large
extent of the license of their customs. Love remains
fertile only so long as it restrains and limits itself.
Christianity, by subjecting men's customs to disci-
pline—one of its noblest services to mankind—succeeded for centuries in maintaining in Europe and
America an incessant fertility, which has proved to be
one of the most potent causes of the increase of our
power."

the burdens of parenthood, in other words, if not best endowed with ability. It is reliably estimated that at the present time one-fourth of the married population produce one-half of the next generation, and there is much evidence to show that a large proportion of this prolific one-fourth is made up of individuals of mediocre, if not defective, natural endowments.

The problem of positive eugenics becomes, therefore, how society can encourage its better endowed men and women to contribute more than their proportion to the next generation. In other words, how it can encourage marriage and parenthood among the truly better elements of society. Here, again, the eugenics movement is beset by many practical difficulties. It has been suggested that the state, in certain instances, should compensate parents for the birth and rearing of children. It has often been truly said that the mother who bears and rears children is serving the state not less than the soldier who serves upon the battle field. Hence we hear a great deal about public pensions to mothers and "mothers' compensation." There can be no doubt, of course, about the service to society of a mother who bears and rears normal children. The only question is whether such a service as this should be compensated in a financial way. Are we going to put every service which individuals render to society upon a monetary basis? Or, are there not some services which we cannot pay adequately for with money? and which we should not attempt to pay for with money because it degrades them? Is not parenthood such a service? Would not the women who would accept compensation for motherhood be the very sort of women whom we might least desire to be mothers? Of course society should not penalize marriage and parenthood on the part of its men and women of ability, through industrial, political or other arrangements, as it doubtless does, to some extent, at the present time. It should not, for example, produce a "reversal of selection" by such economic and social arrangements as to make marriage among its educated classes practically impossible before the age of thirty or as to make celibacy almost a practical necessity for some among them. But, on the other hand, society cannot safely enter upon any pecuniary method of encouraging marriage and parenthood even among those elements that might meet the test of certain qualifications, because such methods would defeat the very end at which they are aimed.[54]

We, then, must give up for the present, at least, the idea of the encouragement of parenthood in any material way. The whole question, therefore, of positive eugenics reduces itself at once to the question of the ideals of life which we should encourage in the young. It, therefore, becomes primarily

[54] This must not be taken to mean the condemnation of the practice of advanced nations in remitting a certain amount of taxation to families where there are children under a certain age, or the practice of granting "maternal benefits" in industrial insurance schemes, such as that of Great Britain. The condemnation is only of *direct* pecuniary methods of encouraging marriage and parenthood.

a matter of education rather than of legislation. The question involved is evidently that of moral education along the lines of sex, marriage, and the family. A large part of the programme of the eugenist must be to induce young people, as Dr. C. B. Davenport says, "to make a more reasonable selection of marriage mates; to fall in love intelligently." This means, of course, that young men and women must, even at a very early age, be given right ideals of marriage and parenthood. If they are to make a more reasonable selection of mates, not only must the widest acquaintance between young people be encouraged by society, but they must also be given other standards of selection than most of them have at the present time. The ideals of good manners, social popularity, good looks, and wealth, must be replaced with the ideals of health, intellectual ability, and moral character. When these latter qualities come to be put first in the mutual choice of the sexes in marriage, there can be no doubt that the benefit to society will be incalculable.

However, something more than the development of right ideals in our young people regarding marriage is necessary for the programme of positive eugenics. That something more is education for parenthood. We hear much of education for good citizenship, but is not a most important part of good citizenship the right fulfilling of the duties and responsibilities of parenthood? By education for parenthood, we mean not so much education in the care and rearing of young children, important as that may be, but, also, instruction of the proper sort along the lines of heredity, sex morality, and the social importance of the family. Hitherto, such education has been mainly left to the family itself, but, on account of the fact that many families do not function educationally in this matter, it would seem necessary to introduce, in a wise way, some of this instruction in our public schools, from the kindergarten up. At any rate, there can be no question that some public educational agency must supplement the home along these lines. Of course, the Church, as the institution charged with the conservation and propagation of moral ideals in society, is best fitted to be this agency; only the Church fails to reach great masses of our population, and as yet is not fully awake to its duties along these lines. Sir Francis Galton's opinion, indeed, was that the eugenics movement could scarcely reach the masses without the development of a eugenic religion. Eugenic religions have already existed, to some extent, in the past, notably Judaism. Christianity, with its doctrine of the love of humanity and the service of man, ought to be especially fitted to aid a rational eugenics programme in modern society. At any rate, eugenics cannot succeed without the development of a eugenic conscience, and such a conscience can best be developed in the masses probably through the aid of religious agencies.

We must, then, give an important place to the eugenics movement in the solution of the social problem. It has insisted upon certain vital truths which society cannot afford to

ignore, and it has brought a great, new hope
into the world. As an undergraduate the
writer was told in his course in sociology that
heredity was a factor beyond human control;
that the most man might aspire to was the
control over certain forces in the environment. Such a statement was perhaps justified
at the time; but the progress of scientific
knowledge of heredity and the rise of the
eugenics movement give grounds for the hope
that mankind may yet exercise in some degree
a rational control over its own heredity; may,
in other words, intelligently modify the qualities of the race itself, rather than leave these
to be determined simply by the blind forces
of physical nature.

Moreover, the moral aspects of the eugenics
movement must not be overlooked. Its whole
trend is to place marriage and the family
upon a much higher basis than it has hitherto
had in human society; upon a basis, not of
the mere individual happiness of the married
parties, but of service of "the humanity which
is to be." The eugenics movement is, there-

143

fore, decidedly humanitarian; and if society will heed its message, it will find its life in every way more normal and "the social problem" much more easy of solution.

The importance of the physical elements in the social life is manifest. We cannot have an A1 society with C3 physical men or even exhausted natural resources. In the rebuilding of our civilization, then, such things as sound heredity, health, sanitation, physical training, proper food, the conservation and development of natural resources must be considered basic. They are not themselves civilization, but they are the foundation upon which it is built. And civilization cannot be higher or stabler than these basic elements permit. In social reconstruction we must not forget the foundations of the social life which these physical elements along with the economic elements about to be discussed constitute.

CHAPTER IV

ECONOMIC ELEMENTS IN THE SOCIAL PROBLEM

FOR more than a century social thought in Western civilization has been predominantly economic. The consciousness of the social problem among the mass of the people has been very largely in economic terms. To a certain extent this attitude of the popular mind is no doubt justifiable. The importance of the economic element in the social problem of to-day, at any rate, is so large that we cannot even begin to understand the problem without understanding the economic conditions which have played such a large part in creating it. We shall attempt, therefore, in this chapter to make a brief analysis of this element and to correlate it with the other elements involved in our problem of social reconstruction.

The importance of the economic element in the social problem has, indeed, given rise to one of the peculiar philosophies of the present, a philosophy which interprets the whole of human living in predominantly economic terms. This is the social philosophy which is ordinarily called "economic determinism" or "historical materialism," though it has also a number of other names. Not only is this social philosophy preached at the present time from the housetops, having been made a part of the creed of a great political party, but it is too often taught from the professor's chair in our leading institutions of learning. Thus we find an eminent American sociologist saying that the spiritual part of civilization "does not need to be specially fostered;" that with suitable material and economic conditions it requires no special attention, but will come to full bloom of itself if given these conditions.[55] This view, of course, implies that the ideas, ideals, and values which make civilization, as we have seen, are entirely determined in their development by economic conditions. While no sociologist who sets out to interpret

[55] Ward, *Pure Sociology*, p. 18.

human history with this view can long adhere
to it consistently, yet, unfortunately, these
views come to be taken up by the mass of
men who build upon them equally one-sided
practical programmes. "Make economic conditions right," they cry, "and other things
will take care of themselves." The *laissez-
faire* attitude of the social philosophy of the
early nineteenth century has entirely broken
down with reference to economic conditions;
but it has not yet broken down in some classes
with reference to other social conditions.
These classes find in economic determinism an
easy refuge from assuming social responsibility
and control over *all* the conditions of life.

We are very far, indeed, from asserting that
this popular social philosophy of the present
has not a large element of truth in it; nor is it
difficult to discover just the measure of its
truth. There can be no doubt that many of
the main features of modern civilization have
really been determined by our present industrial system. The way in which people

get their living has in all ages been a most influential factor in their general living. The methods of producing and distributing wealth, in other words, must in the very nature of things greatly influence the whole culture of a people. In a certain sense the dependence of man upon economic conditions in the strict sense, indeed, increases as civilization advances; for through the labour of countless generations and through the force of tradition and established institutions, the economic environment comes to have a good deal of the same relation to civilized man that the geographic environment had to primitive man. We know how largely primitive man was a slave of geographic conditions; so, too, modern man is so dependent upon his economic surroundings that we cannot conceive of him existing apart from them. But, to repeat the illustration used in Chapter III, to say that we could not live if the sun should cease to exist is very different from saying that the sun determines all of our goings and comings. In other words, we may cordially acknowledge the complete dependence of civilized man upon the economic system under which he lives without acknowledging that that system *determines*, even in the long run, all his ways of feeling, thinking, and acting.[56]

Just what part of modern civilization, then, does the economic element determine? It is not difficult to answer. The most ordinary superficial observation shows that our economic system determines the great outline, the framework, so to speak, of our civilization. For example, the modern great city is almost entirely a product of modern industry. The sixteenth and seventeenth centuries scarcely knew such cities. Not until the industrial revolution began to make itself felt toward the end of the eighteenth century did cities begin greatly to multiply. At the beginning of the nineteenth century scarce four per cent of the population of the United States lived

[56] For a more elaborate discussion of economic determinism see the writer's article on "Marx's Economic Determinism in the Light of Modern Psychology" in the *American Journal of Sociology*, July, 1911.

in cities, while in 1910 over forty per cent lived under urban conditions and nearly one-fourth of the population were dwellers in fifty great cities. One predominant trait of modern civilization, the tendency to develop sharply contrasting urban and rural populations, undoubtedly owes its existence to the rise of our present economic system. For when we examine the causes of the growth of cities, it becomes clearly apparent that these causes are almost wholly economic. The industrial revolution which came through the invention of labour-saving machines transferred industry, as we have seen, from the home and the workshop to the factory. Economic reasons compel the grouping of these factories at certain strategic points in the highways of trade and commerce, while specialization of factories, communities and even nations in various branches of industry increased commerce and multiplied the population engaged in commerce at the same points. Almost simultaneously the application of labour-saving machinery and of scientific methods to agriculture liberated vast numbers of men from the soil. These had to find employment elsewhere and they found it in the manufacturing and commerce of the city. Not the love of amusement, nor facilities for education and culture have been responsible, in a word, for the growth of our cities, but certain compelling economic necessities of our time.

Now, the city has come to dominate Western civilization. It touches the life and character of everyone, no matter whether he lives in the city or in the rural districts. The city of the present gives a certain form and character, therefore, to our whole civilization, both urban and rural. This is equivalent to saying that the economic conditions which have given rise to the city have touched life at every point. Illustrations of a similar nature could be indefinitely multiplied with reference to other features of our civilization. But when we have conceded that modern industry has shaped the main outlines of our civilization, that is not sufficient warrant for concluding that our industrial system determines everything in our social life. On the contrary, it needs but little investigation to show that there are many intimate personal relations between individuals which are very far from being determined by the economic system under which we live. Men still think and feel and act in these intimate relations not so differently from what they did long before the present economic system was born. Many of the ideas, ideals, and values by which men live, in other words, far antedate our present economic system, and will probably survive long after it is dead. It is not true, therefore, that the spiritual elements in life, and especially not those contained in moral, religious, and artistic ideas and ideals, are determined by methods of producing and distributing wealth. The economic system constrains us and even has, as we shall see, a seductive influence upon our ideas and ideals, but it does not and it cannot enchain the soul of man.

Nevertheless, our economic system is so intimately wrapped up with the modern social problem, as we have already said, that there is no solution of that problem unless we can provide a better industrial system than the present world has yet realized. It may be that what the world needs most of all is a new spirit, a new system of values, but it cannot get this new spirit in any adequate or complete way until it has a new industrial system. Our present system of industry, in other words, is such that it hampers and restricts the social and spiritual development of mankind. The sooner this is recognized and understood, the better it will be for the world. Just as human slavery at a certain period came to be a stumbling block to all further progress, so modern capitalism has come to be a similar stumbling block.

The present economic order, which we may call that of capitalistic industry, came in, as we have seen, with the industrial revolution; when the invention of machinery and the development of the factory system made it no longer possible for the working man to have the same freedom and independence which he once enjoyed, when he owned the tools of his industry and perhaps the little shop in which he worked. The invention of labour-saving machinery was, to be sure, an epoch-making step in the progress of mankind, but because of the costliness of this machinery and of the great factory in which it was installed, it inevitably robbed, for a time, at least, the working man of a large part of his economic liberty; and it placed industry in the hands of the wealthy who could supply the capital which was necessary to carry it on under the factory system. Thus was modern capitalism born. Now, what we are concerned to point out is that modern capitalism must not be confused with the wage-earning system. It has sometimes been said that we have capitalism wherever one man works for another. But if this is true, capitalism has existed since the dawn of civilization. All social life necessitates that one man work for another and from very early times men have worked for wages. *Capitalism*, in the true sense in which we shall use the term,

154

exists only where such vast aggregations of capital are necessary to carry on a given line of industry that in that line the working men become practically dependent upon the wealthy capitalistic class. But these conditions have beome so general in the modern world that all Western civilization can now be said to represent a capitalistic society. Capitalism, at any rate, dominates our present civilization.

But what are the objections to capitalism? Why must it be regarded as a stumbling block to the higher social and moral development of mankind? The reply is that there are certain characteristic features of capitalism *as it at present exists in society* which constitute such a damaging indictment against it that the most thoughtful students of social conditions everywhere are uniting in condemning it.

In the first place, capitalism leads to the exploitation of labour, that is the selfish use of one man by another. It is often said that the way to get rich is to get other people to work for you. If, however, other people received a just compensation for their labour, a just wage, covering practically the product of their labour, no one would get rich very rapidly this way. What is meant is, that under present conditions it is easily possible for the rich and economically successful in society to get the economically weak to work for them under such conditions that they need not pay them a full compensation for the service they render. This is all the easier, not only because of the dependence of the economically weak, but because moral standards have traditionally sanctioned such practices. It is considered simply good business to hire labour in as cheap a market as can be found; to pay no more to the labouring man than what is barely necessary under a system of competitive bidding of labouring men against one another. Hence, the tendency has been often to force wages down to what was necessary for the bare subsistence of the labouring man and his family. Indeed, wages have tended to go lower than that and to establish themselves in some instances upon what is known as the single man's standard.

Another objection to capitalism is that it results in an unjust distribution of wealth. From the very fact that it gives undue opportunities for the exploitation of labour it must result in certain wealth going to the employing class, which justly belongs to the labouring class. Now, there can be no doubt at all but that if we take the labouring class as a whole in modern industrial communities, they are not adequately paid for their work. It is estimated that in the United States, for example, where wages are higher than in any other advanced industrial nation, sixty-five per cent of the labourers receive wages of less than six hundred dollars a year. On the other hand, according to the figures of the United States Census, the profits in manufacturing industry in the year 1909 were about twelve per cent after due allowance for interest, insurance, taxes and all other fixed charges on the total capital employed. In other words, the capitalist class received in addition to "interest" in manufacturing industry in 1909, about twelve per cent of "profits." On the other hand, only a little over fifty-one per cent of the total value of the product added by manufacturing went to working men and other employees in the form of wages or salaries. It will be seen from these figures, even though they are by no means accurate, that the working man is still very far from receiving a just share of the product of his labour; and that, on the other hand, the comparatively small class of owners receive in addition to the interest on their capital a considerable margin of "speculative profit."

Now, there may be some question raised as to the rightfulness of interest, and this question is, of course, already raised by the socialists and many other types of radical social thinkers. But what shall we say of the element of "speculative profit" which is now going to the capitalist class? If there is any question to be raised as to the legitimacy of interest, much more could it be raised of this element of so-called private profit. We may assume that interest, wages of superintendence, and the like, are a part of "necessary profits," without which business cannot be carried on upon a basis of private ownership and initiative. But "speculative profits" are not "necessary profits" and they represent in no sense a compensation for services rendered to the community. The whole modern industrial world, however, has become so accustomed to looking upon speculative profits as justly belonging to the owner or proprietor of a business that it refuses to think that business can be carried on upon any other basis. A large proportion of the business of the world, however, has always been carried on without any elements of speculative profit in it. It has had to remain satisfied with necessary profits, interest and wages of superintendence, in other words, with adequate compensation for service rendered. If business were for service and not for private profit, there would be no element of speculative profits demanded by the capitalist class.

Whether the capitalist class is entitled to interest or not, is probably a question concerning which there will be many debates in the future. But it would seem safe to say at the present time that the capitalist class is certainly not entitled to "speculative profits" in the same sense or degree even to which it is entitled to "interest"; and that if for reasons of public policy speculative gains are allowed to go to private individuals they cannot regard themselves as entitled to them in the same sense in which they are entitled to property got by service rendered the community. We must distinguish, in other words, between "earnings" and "findings" in the income of all classes, and speculative profit is certainly "a finding."

Now, the result of the appropriation of these "findings" or speculative profits by the capitalist class is the enormous enrichment of the capitalist class and the poverty of the labouring class. Poverty, to be sure, is not the greatest evil in the world, as so many of the writers of the present assume. Poverty, indeed, is not an evil at all when the circumstances are such that one can readily raise one's self out of poverty. But this is not the case with modern industrial poverty. Much of the poverty of the modern world, in other words, is of the hopeless sort, from which strong and capable individuals cannot extricate themselves. Now, hopeless poverty is not only depressing but easily becomes positively demoralizing to the individual. It robs him not only of hope but also of the higher moral aspirations of life. Thus poverty which is hopeless becomes degrading and becomes linked with degeneracy, vice, and crime. With our easy theory that every one can look out for himself, and that rich and poor alike are entitled to all that they can get and all that they can keep, we have thus allowed to grow up in Western civilization a propertyless labouring class who have no interest in the future, for they are without hope that they can extricate themselves from their present position save by revolution.

Another result of this unjust distribution

of wealth which capitalism has brought about is the breeding of war between the classes in society, between the propertied on the one hand and the propertyless on the other. Now, class war is not a normal thing in a properly organized human society; but it is an ominous and an almost omnipresent thing in Western civilization. Sympathy and goodwill unite men in harmonious social life, but hatred and antagonism dissolve all social bonds. Unless we can overcome the class antagonism which is growing up, we must come, sooner or later, to open and bloody conflicts in Western nations between the labouring and the capitalistic class. From that conflict, as we have already insisted, it is improbable that a higher and more stable civilization would issue.

So, too, capitalism has needlessly increased the antagonism between nations.[57] Through

[57] That capitalism tends to peace is, of course, often asserted, and it should not be ignored that capitalism of a certain type may tend strongly to preserve peace between nations. This is capitalism of the conservative or "investment" type which has given up "speculative

their control of government, the capitalist class in Western civilization have often used the machinery of the State to promote their own interests. They have demanded new markets for their goods and immense armaments to protect trade and commerce, and have not scrupled to use Machiavellian statecraft to reach their ends. They have thus bred war and the spirit of war between nations. The Great War between European nations again shows this. While we have insisted upon the deep moral causes of the Great War, as due in last analysis to conflicting traditions and ideals of life in Western civilization, and while socialism we believe to be no guarantee against either national egoism or moral atavism; yet it would be most unjust to overlook the obvious truth that the war enterprise." But, on the other hand, capitalism of the "exploitative" type is continually giving rise to bickerings and jealousies between nations. And it is not unfair to say that the capitalism of the speculative, "exploitative" type has hitherto dominated in Western civilization, and has had a large share in *provoking* many wars, among them the present one.

has also been due to the long development of an intense economic rivalry between the two great capitalistic nations—Great Britain and Germany, in both of which the government has been for a long period more or less dominated by the capitalist class. The older capitalism of England looked with suspicion upon the newer capitalism of Germany with its bid for the markets of the world. This led British capitalism to use the resources of British diplomacy and prestige to block the commercial and political expansion of Germany in Africa and Asia; while, on the other hand, the military-capitalist class of Germany, backed by an astounding philosophy of national and racial egoism, slowly fanned into the flame of war the slumbering fires of the hatred arising from the economic antagonism of the two nations. Wars existed of course before the capitalistic system and they will probably exist after it; but it would be foolish to deny that capitalism, particularly of the

[59] See Hayes, *A Political and Social History of Modern Europe*, Part V.

"exploitative" type, tends to breed war between nations as well as between classes.

Now that peace has come again, we can see more clearly than ever how commercial imperialism and the exploitative capitalism which seeks to dominate the markets and the natural resources of the world lead to war. For it was these which led to such disagreements among the Allies at the Paris Peace Conference that the peace treaty finally adopted by the Conference was such a compromise that we may well fear that it lays the foundations for future wars.

Now, it is time that we give up the fallacy of thinking that peace can be fostered by war, whether between classes or between nations. Hatred breeds hatred and war breeds war. A general conflict between the propertied and the propertyless in Western civilization could only mean its death knell. It would be far more terrible than the Great World War of 1914–1918. The growth of class antagonism and of class hate should, therefore, reconcile the wealthy classes in society to giving up a part of their private property if nothing else can; for this growing gulf between the rich and the poor must rend our civilization asunder if it continues.

A third objection to capitalism is that it fosters materialism in both the rich and the poor and thus chokes out the higher life of the spirit. Capitalism fosters materialism in the rich because, with their gains from private profit, every avenue of luxury and self-indulgence is open to them. The very acceptance of private profit, indeed, of the doctrine that one is entitled to all one can get within the law, means that the sense of social responsibility will become blunted, if not obliterated. At the same time, the enormous growth of wealth in the capitalist class leads to the undermining of character in other insidious ways. Men come to trust in riches, they come to think themselves above both human and divine law. This world's pleasures and enjoyments loom so large that they seem the only good worth striving for. Men become materialists in their ideals and theories of life as well as in their practices. Religion loses its meaning except as a badge of respectability, and the higher reality of spiritual things is either denied or receives simply a conventional acquiescence. It is truly hard for these people to enter "the Kingdom of Heaven."

As has been well said, "The lust of personal wealth and the prevailing fever leave men with no eyes for what is worthy or base in civilization. Provided they can make their own homes pleasant and decorate them with a certain measure of taste, they will contemplate in comfort cities which have no single public building worthy of the name and populations squalid and ill-clothed. It is not iron or engines, it is the unchecked operation of greed that makes life so hideous; and until the soul of man is weary of his millions we need hardly look for much improvement." [60]

Capitalism fosters materialism not less among the poor than among the rich, because it makes the standard of all worth financial success. The doings and the standards of

[60] Figgis, *Civilization at the Cross Roads,* p. 104.

the capitalist class are therefore looked up to by the poor as the life which secretly, at least, they would like to copy if they could. The standards of the labouring man thus also become almost wholly materialistic. He may wish for a juster distribution of wealth, but largely for the sake of being "better off" rather than for the sake of being "better." The hopeless poverty, moreover, of the least fortunate elements of the labouring class makes it difficult, if not impossible, for them to believe in the worth of spiritual things. Therefore, the net result of capitalism is to exalt purely economic and materialistic standards of living in all classes in society.

Our indictment against capitalism as it exists in its present form in society might be almost indefinitely continued. We have mentioned these three chief indictments, that it leads to the exploitation of labour, that it results in an unjust distribution of wealth, and that it fosters materialistic standards of happiness and living, because we believe

that these are the strongest indictments that
can be brought. They are sufficiently strong
to lead all sensible men these days to condemn
capitalism as it at present exists in Western
civilization. Thus far the reader may agree
with our diagnosis of the situation. It is
easier, however, to diagnose a social situation
than it is to suggest a remedy for the evils
found. While the reader may agree with
our diagnosis, he may disagree with the
remedy which is about to be suggested. If
the remedy is one which may be easily criti-
cized, that should surprise no one who understands at all the present condition of the social
sciences, because in the present condition of
our scientific knowledge regarding human
society only a fool or a partisan (and the terms,
perhaps, are nearly synonymous) would be
certain that he knew the specific remedy for
any grave social evil. And yet certain things
can be pointed out which may lead us to hope
that the situation is not so desperate as it
seems. It must not be expected, of course,
that the evils of capitalism which have grown

up through four or five generations can be eradicated in a day, or that a new and higher phase of industrial organization, in which justice and liberty shall be realized, can be inaugurated over night. The present generation, above all, needs to be patient and test each step that is taken rather than to rush into some hasty revolutionary change the effects of which cannot well be foreseen.

It would seem that the way out is, in the main, along lines which are now already beginning to be tested, namely, along the lines of assuming fuller social responsibility for our industrial situation and fuller social control over all industrial processes, and not in the speedy abolition of private ownership and initiative in certain great lines of economic activity. To be sure, public ownership, wherever it is advantageous and at the same time practicable, should be welcome, because public ownership is the fullest expression of social control and social responsibility over industrial processes. We want all the public

170

ownership and management, in other words, which we are really ready for; but the question remains, How much are we ready for? It is also a question whether many of the advantages of public ownership cannot be secured in our great industries without destroying private ownership and private initiative.

For private ownership and private initiative have their advantages too, as must be acknowledged even by the most radical socialists who understand anything of human nature and human society. Private ownership in some sense, indeed, is as necessary for human society as the private home. As Professor Small says, "Anyone who has read the ten commandments carefully knows that private property is written in between their lines." The institution of private property has, indeed, been one of the foundations of civilization itself, and the tradition of private property must be preserved as one of the corner stones of social order.[61] *The objection*

[61] For an excellent discussion of the whole question of private property, its evolution and social value, see the

is not to private property, but to the abuses of private property which capitalism has fostered. Still the question remains whether large business shall be public or private; [62] and if we decide that there are advantages in retaining private ownership in any particular case, then there is a question whether we cannot secure in many cases the advantages of public ownership and retain private ownership too.

It seems to the writer that there is little question that this latter can be done, provided we can secure proper governmental machinery and proper ethical ideals and spirit among our people, particularly among the possessing classes. We have need only to carry the programme of social regulation and control both

recent work (1913) on *Property, Its Duties and Rights,* by Professor Hobhouse, Professor Bartlet, Dr. A. J. Carlyle and others (published by Macmillan and Company).

[62] For an illuminating discussion of the relations between public and private property in modern society, see Professor Ely's just published work on *Property and Contract in their Relations to the Distribution of Wealth,* two volumes (1914).

by government and public sentiment very
much farther than what we have already done
in order to achieve this. We must, in other
words, regulate big business and little business
from beginning to end in the interest of the
public. We must insist that *business is for
social service and not for private profit*. And
this means that we must insist that business
of all sorts shall be so carried on as to do justice, and not injustice, to the working man,
as well as to the public at large.

But the working man, it may be said, lives
upon such a small income, with such a narrow
economic surplus at best, that his position remains precarious no matter how much business may be regulated. But if business is to
be based upon the idea of service then *business
must furnish adequate protection to the working
man in his precarious condition*. This means
that the whole programme of scientific social
betterment which our social workers have
favoured must be carried out.[63] We must first

[63] An excellent statement of this programme is to
be found in Devine's *Misery and Its Causes*, Chap. VI.

of all have strict regulation by law of the hours and conditions of employment in accordance with the highest hygienic and moral standards. We must then have adequate insurance against the contingencies of life, such as sickness, accident, unemployment, old age, and invalidity. We must also provide an adequate relief system for those whom this insurance system cannot protect, such as the weak, the defective, and the inefficient. We must have such measures as the minimum wage, or a living wage for all who work. Free employment bureaus, or labour exchanges, should exist in every city. Free justice should be furnished in our courts of law, without any intermediation of lawyers, where small amounts are involved, or disputes between the labourer and his employer. This would only place the working man on a level of equality with his employer; for hitherto the expenses of our law courts have been such that only the comparatively well-to-do could afford to appeal to them for justice. Free industrial training for trades of all sorts should be provided in our public school system for those who wish to enter industry. Finally, the working man must be protected in his right to organize for purposes of mutual aid and collective bargaining, in such a way, however, that he shall not be encouraged to infringe upon the rights of his less fortunate, unorganized brother. In brief, social justice must be assured to the economically weak in society.

"But where is all the money coming from to carry out this ambitious programme of the social worker?" the objector may ask. The reply is that in the wealthier Western nations there is ample money to carry out such a humanitarian programme toward the workers without laying additional burdens upon any who are not perfectly able to carry them. Some of the money for such a programme of social and industrial justice might well come through private philanthropy, but undoubtedly the larger amount of such funds should be raised by public taxation of those who are able to bear it. We must, in other words, have such reforms in our systems of taxation as will furnish adequate revenue for social needs and serve at the same time to distribute wealth and economic opportunity more evenly in society. *Scientific reform of taxation is probably the most important administrative method by which the injustices and inequalities of our present economic system can be overcome.*

Now, as we pointed out above, legitimate incomes under our present system of property rights, may be roughly divided into "earnings" and "findings"; and as we have seen, one's right to "findings" can scarcely be considered as on the same moral and social plane as one's right to "earnings." If society permits "findings" to pass mainly into the pocketbooks of private individuals rather than into the public purse, it can only be upon the basis of temporary social expediency. Now, it is just these "findings" which progressive tax reformers propose shall carry the main burdens of taxation in modern states. No doubt it will be one of the nice points of the statesmanship of the future to determine what are "findings" and what are "earnings," what are "earned" incomes and what "unearned" in our industrial system. Without entering upon any attempt to make a nice distinction between the two, it is sufficient to point out that the economically fortunate classes in present society have manifestly many sources of "unearned income." One of these for example is the income from bequests and inheritances. While the principle of the solidarity of the family is so important in society that the law may properly exempt from taxation such bequests among its members as will reasonably tend to secure their economic adjustment and to prevent destitution, yet above this minimum, as indeed most modern states recognize, there should be a progressively increasing rate of taxation, which should be at least doubled in the case of collateral inheritances. There is no reason why in the case of very large bequests to private individuals the rate of taxation should not be much heavier than it is in any modern state.

177

Another source of unearned income which the economically fortunate enjoy is the "unearned increment" in land values, which spring from the scarcity of land relative to the population. This is best seen in our rapidly growing great cities where, on account of the scarcity of land, the speculative profit on "real estate deals" which consist of the purchase and sale of lots is frequently enormous, and in the high "ground rents" of such cities. There is no good reason why all this "unearned increment" should go into the private purses of the real estate speculator or the landlord class, and some of the most progressive communities of the world are beginning to make this also a source of public revenue.

Another source of unearned income is the "speculative profits" which come in certain lines of business because of some temporary or permanent social advantage which that line has. These cases spring not only from "natural monopoly," the granting of "franchises," and the like, but from many social conditions. It is exceedingly desirable that such "speculative profits" should also be taxed. Probably a general graduated "income tax" is best suited to make the finder of such "findings" share them with society, while it has the additional great social advantage of reaching unearned incomes in present society which come from interest on fortunes accumulated through the unearned increment in land values, from "speculative profits,' or even from fraudulent practices, passed on, perhaps, from one generation to another by bequest. Now that the graduated income tax with proper administrative machinery has proved its entire practicability in the leading countries of the civilized world, the chief question concerning it can only be that of its limits. The tax upon the larger incomes would not seem to be yet in any country sufficiently high to affect materially the distribution of wealth. At any rate, it is well said that this form of taxation has come to stay if civilization continues to progress; and probably the only change which will be made in it in the future will be to make it higher for the higher incomes.

The proper taxation of inheritances, of incomes, and of monopoly land values will then produce sufficient revenue to meet all public needs in carrying out a constructive programme of social betterment. Inasmuch as these taxes cannot be shifted when properly administered,[64] and inasmuch as they have already been put into operation in high degree in the most progressive nations, the objection which might be raised to them would seem to be largely academic, or of a general sociological nature. If it be said, for example, that modern States are not to be trusted with such huge funds, that they would not be used for public good, but would become sources of political corruption, or would be squandered on immense military and naval equipments; then the heavy burden rests upon their op-

[64] The scientific principles of taxation may be consulted by the reader in the works of leading economists, especially in the works of Professor E. R. A. Seligman.

ponent of showing that they would be so misused. On the contrary, the very existence of
a social programme calling for vast expendi-
tures for public welfare would seem to be the
surest guarantee that public funds would not
be squandered on armaments, or dissipated
through political corruption.

The stock argument, however, against modern states entering upon a progressive programme of social and industrial betterment,
and of levying upon some of the economic
surplus of the economically fortunate to
finance the same, is that it would "hurt business." It will discourage investment if all
the "findings" in modern business above
"earnings" have to be shared with the public.
The wealthy classes will sulk; they prefer no
return on their money rather than the chance
of mere legitimate interest. In brief, "capital" will go on a "strike."

Now, there has been abundant evidence in
the history of modern business that just this
thing might happen. Indeed, so long as the
ethical basis of business remains arrant egoism

or mere self-interest, it is the thing which probably will happen. But if business is put upon the basis of social service, it is highly improbable that "capital will go on a strike" because its chances of profits have to be lowered to meet social needs. The example of "business as usual" without material enhancement of prices though profits may be enormously curtailed, in a country aflame with patriotic feeling during a war, shows this. Here comes in again, in other words, the disturbing spiritual factor in the form of an ethical standard which may rule an entire class or an entire people. As long as political economy could base itself upon a purely egoistic theory of human nature—upon pure self-interest—it was possible to ignore largely the influence of the ethical standards of classes upon business. But now that modern psychology has shown such a theory of human nature to be false, and that altruism is as natural to man as egoism, the possibility of controlling even business by altruistic ideals, in some degree at least, must be admitted as entirely within the field of a practicable social programme.

Hence, the reply to those who say that a programme of full social justice to the workers would "hurt business" is that if business were conducted upon the proper ethical basis— upon the basis of the service of society—it would hurt no legitimate business. This means practically, however, that the wealthy classes must content themselves with a smaller income return on the capital which society permits them to hold and manage in trust, as it were, for the benefit of humanity. They must, in other words, be willing to give up a considerable part of their unearned income to the State and to private philanthropy; and if the rest is to be used for the development of legitimate business, they must also give up their luxury and self-indulgence.

If it be said that this is expecting too much of the economically fortunate classes, the reply is that such sacrifice for the common good is only in accordance with the ethical principles which many of them have long professed—the Christian doctrine of the stewardship of wealth. It is also in accord with the doctrine of social obligation which scientific social ethics reveals as springing from the facts of social science. "We must recognize," says Mr. Seebohm Rowntree, a wealthy British manufacturer, "that if justice is to be done to the workers, it will mean sacrifice on the part of the rich. *The poverty at one end of the social scale will not be removed except by encroaching heavily upon the great riches at the other end.*" [65] Fortunately many of the best American men of wealth have expressed themselves in similar terms.

Another objection sometimes raised to a programme of industrial justice supported by taxation is that it would dry up the springs of private benevolence and of spontaneous brotherly help between man and man. It would reduce everything to the dead level of law and of governmental coercion. But this would surely not necessarily be so. In a

[65] Quoted by Henderson, *Social Programmes of the West*, p. 129.

democratic society, ruled sufficiently by humanitarian ideals to enter upon and support a programme of social justice, there would be no lack of spontaneous expressions of sympathy and brotherhood between man and man. In any case the aim of a rational private philanthropy can only be to render itself less and less necessary. It is desirable that brotherhood in society should exhibit itself in justice even more than in charity, as the latter is commonly conceived.

As to the internal organization of industry, it is evident from all that has been said that it should be more democratic, fraternal, and coöperative—less "capitalistic." Labour can no longer be treated as a "commodity"; it must be treated human. The employer and the employee must recognize that they are partners in the performance of a common public service. All this means that the employees must have a voice in the conduct of the business—that they must have some reasonable control over the conditions under which they work. This can be accomplished, perhaps, through such devices as Shop Committees and Industrial Councils; but of even more importance is the spirit of democracy and service in both employer and employees.

Finally, it may be said that an economic programme like the above is "socialism," although party socialists will undoubtedly regard it as an academic fancy dictated by overfriendliness to the present capitalistic order. The time should be past, however, for condemning things by mere names. If by "socialism" is meant collective control over all the conditions of social life, then that is what all human history has been aiming at. All sane students of social life are "socialists" in that sense. If, however, by "socialism" is meant the public ownership and management of all capital, or at least of a majority of the business of a country, then the above programme is not "socialism," though so far as the writer can see there is no moral objection to such "socialism" if it is practicable. The historical socialist movement, however, has neither endorsed the philosophical socialism which we first defined, nor been content to

make its programme simply the public ownership and management of business in order that
a higher social life may be realized. On the
contrary, it has had attached to it in most
countries a whole philosophy of the social life,
filled with the dangerous negations which we
have been refuting, such as "economic determinism," the class-conflict theory of society,
and the cataclysmic or "revolution" theory
of social progress. Thus the socialist movement has transformed itself from a constructive movement to a negative one. This must
be regarded as one of the tragedies of human
history, because all this negative social philosophy is no essential part of a true socialism.

The tragedy of socialism has become evident especially through the Great War. In
Russia, in particular, the spirit of Marxian
socialism has been revealed as that of civil
war. There, after a democratic and moderate
socialist government had already been set up,
the extreme Marxians, the Maximalists or
Bolsheviki, overthrew the government by
force and established a "dictatorship of the

proletariat." Not only did they invoke the power of one class against another to right real or fancied wrongs and make the old mistake of trying to organize society upon a basis of force—thus showing the essentially Prussian spirit of Marxism—but they suppressed liberty and interpreted equality as a process of leveling everybody down. As a sympathetic observer said of the similar though less bloody proletarian revolution in Hungary, after personal investigation:[66] "There is no liberty. There is no democracy." Indeed, the socialist state, as Bolshevism has interpreted it, seems to be about as far as possible from that free society which we picture as the social ideal. It is rather inverted autocracy. Yet it is what revolutionary socialism threatens in Western civilization generally.

On the other hand, moderate British socialism, as represented by the British Labour Party, seems to have transformed itself from a negative to a constructive movement, which is non-revolutionary and "experimental" in

[66] *The New Republic*, May 24, 1919, p. 122.

character. In its "Report on Reconstruction," its first principle, it declares, "is the securing to every member of the community, in good times and bad alike (and not only to the strong and able, the well born or the fortunate), of all the requisites of healthy life and worthy citizenship." Moreover, the party explicitly repudiates the idea that it is speaking for class interests, or that it aims at the supremacy of one class over another. More remarkable still, it proposes to rely on science to carry out its programme of social and industrial reconstruction. "In all the complexities of politics, the Labour Party," it declares, "stands for increased study, for the scientific investigation of each succeeding problem. . . ."

Here at last is a truly scientific socialism as opposed to the "scientific" dogmatism of Marx and his followers. Such a socialism will necessarily be *experimental* rather than revolutionary in character, and will have as its first step the realization of such a programme of industrial betterment as we have set forth. Whether such a programme is carried through by a socialist party or by other parties, however, matters not. It is manifestly the sole alternative, in the present social situation, to *revolutionary* socialism.

While the labour problem is only a single phase of the social problem, justice to the worker has become the great moral issue of our time. The programme of industrial justice which we have outlined is no mere academic fancy—the product of mere abstract theorizing. It is the actual programme upon which the most advanced Western nations are entering under the guidance of the soundest social thinkers and workers. It has grown out of the perception that the industrial poverty which so menaces our civilization, can be abolished like nearly all social evils, *without revolution*, and that it should be abolished. But those who understand the social problem of the present in its deeper aspects know that this is but a preliminary step, though a most essential one, in organized, scientifically planned social progress. They know that beyond lies the problem of socializing the individual and of conserving and building up the spiritual life of humanity.

CHAPTER V

SPIRITUAL AND IDEAL ELEMENTS IN THE SOCIAL PROBLEM

WHAT the world needs is a new spirit, that is, a new set of values, even more than a new economic system. Indeed, it needs a new economic system chiefly in order that it may get a new spirit; but the two must develop together. Without a new spirit, a new economic system would but serve as another opportunity for the strong to exploit the weak. On the other hand, without a new system of industry it is almost impossible to get new and higher ideals of life among the masses of the people. As long as injustice reigns in the material conditions of life, we must not expect people to believe strongly in the ideals of brotherhood. On the other hand, without an ideal of brotherhood to guide their activity, no group of human beings can realize a brotherly society. But

there is no circle here. Ideas and ideals exist
to guide and control activity; therefore we
must begin our making of the society of to-
morrow with a practical idea of what that
society shall be; and we must have faith in
the power to realize our ideas and ideals.

Nothing is more lamentable than for men
to lose their faith in this power of ideas and
ideals; for, however much we may admit the
influence of other factors, it remains true beyond the gainsaying of all, except of absolute
sceptics, that the intellect has been the active
factor in human progress in the past. While we
are far from endorsing any ideological theory of
history, yet ideas and values have ever been,
since civilization began, the chief instruments
by which man has controlled his adjustments
to his fellow man. Such ideas as the fatherhood of God, the brotherhood of man, and
the right of the individual to liberty, have had
the utmost influence in shaping human history in the past. It will not do to say that
such ideas have been derived from the physical and economic environment; for they have

sprung quite as much from the instincts and native tendencies of human nature as from the influence of any factors in the environ- ment. When men ascribe the origin of ideas to various influences in the environment, they forget the part played by human instincts, by the creative imagination, and by construc- tive reasoning. They forget, in other words, that the mind of man is self-active and needs no compulsion from without. They have com- mitted the fallacy of accepting as a theory of human nature a passive psychology which is utterly discredited by science to-day. Thus economic determinism, or any other material- istic theory of human progress, is without scientific foundation.

But even more must the society of to-morrow be made by spiritual and ideal elements than the society of yesterday, because in the more complex stages of social evolution the spiritual factors have an ever greater part to play. Science and education must become the chief means of controlling and reorganizing the society of the future. A clear understanding of our social life will alone make possible its highest development. However, it is only when the discoveries of science and the conclusions of reflective thought are formulated into standards, that is, transmuted into values, that their social efficacy will become apparent. In other words, we can have a right social life only upon a basis of right ideals as to the relations of men to one another. Ideals are judgments as to the value of activities, and they are indispensable instruments in bringing about any high type of adaptation between individuals. We must have, therefore, the right sort of ideals as a basis before we can realize any high type of social life.

Not only must we have right ideals in human society, but the mass of men, one way or another, must be brought to agree upon right ideals. If there is hopeless disagreement in opinions and ideals among individuals, it is idle to suppose that their social life can be characterized by harmony and unity. Now, as we have already seen, the present age is

characterized by an apparently almost hopeless disagreement as to the values and ideals
of life. Conflicting traditions and judgments
among us have divided modern civilization
into warring sects, parties, factions, classes,
and nations. Science, to be sure, is at work
trying to bring men to more unanimity in their
opinions regarding the meaning and ideals
of life. But a preliminary work of social
science must be to point out in the beginning
the importance of ideas and ideals in society
and of agreement respecting them, if we are
to reach any solution of the social problem
at all. In other words, people must come to
realize, even before science can act as their
guide, the importance of ideas and ideals in
practical life, and especially the importance
of conserving those which the experience of
the past has shown to be truly constructive
and productive of harmony and unity in
society.

Unfortunately, however, owing to the strife
between conflicting traditions and interests

in present society, large masses of men have come to take a partially or wholly negative attitude toward the very values which have guided the social development of the past and which have proved the most civilizing agencies. It is not simply that whole masses of men have gone over to the happiness or "self-culture" ideals of life, but we have also people in plenty who advocate, for themselves at least, a return to a primitive animal-like stage of life—people who believe that the gratification of native impulses and appetites constitutes the supreme good of life. We have others in plenty, who, though they may not go so far, yet disbelieve in organized government, morality, or religion. Finally, we have the worshippers of power and success, who, though difficult to enumerate, constitute no small fraction in the most typical communities of Western civilization.

It is a great mistake to think that such negative philosophers as Rousseau, Bakunin, and Nietzsche are simply aberrant, exceptional social types. On the contrary, they represent profound tendencies in the social life of the present. These apostles of social negativism have, in other words, but expressed in their doctrines the socially negative attitude of large classes in Western civilization. This social negativism, moreover, runs through the thought of many of the thinkers whose names have become linked with great modern movements, such as Spencer and Marx. Indeed, our whole social life has become tinctured with the philosophy of individualism on the one hand, which asserts that there is no more unity inherent in our social life than there is in a dog fight; and on the other hand, with the philosophy of materialism or agnosticism, which fails to see any more meaning in our social life than in the growth and development of a colony of bacteria. In ethics and religion, in those most intimate inner matters which concern our social life, we have been busy sowing the wind, and it should not be surprising that we are now beginning to reap the whirlwind.

But, if we acknowledge the importance of

ideas and ideals, of the spiritual element in life, then what policy must we pursue to conserve our spiritual possessions and to transmit them unimpaired to the society of the future? Without going into details it is evident that modern civilization has suffered its spiritual possessions in a number of lines to decay, and that we must now enter upon a policy of conservation of these spiritual values, if there is to be any chance of realizing a humanity adjusted to the requirements of a higher social existence. At least along four lines Western peoples have been failing to conserve their higher ideals, namely, along the lines of the family, of government, of religion, and of morality.

If our civilization is to extricate itself from its present anarchy, we must have a revaluation of family life. The place of the family in human society, as a natural intermediary between individualism and a wider life of social service, must be evident to all who have reflected upon the matter impartially. Not only does the child receive in the family in the simplest, most direct and most effective way, those traditions regarding industry, government, law, morality, and religion, which are the spiritual possessions of the race, but he also learns in it his first lessons in love, service, and self-sacrifice. Loyalty and unselfish devotion to the larger human groups, psychology shows, cannot be effectively developed without first developing loyalty to those smaller groups which call forth the instinctive affections of the child.[67] The attachments developed in the family make possible and actually strengthen the attachments to larger groups. Hence where family sentiments are strong, there one usually finds strong patriotism and strong social sympathies in general.

In other words, the individual learns in the family the meaning and the reality of social solidarity, and he gets necessarily from the family life many of his ideals for the social

[67] See Royce, *The Philosophy of Loyalty*, especially, pp. 220–8.

life generally. Thus the family has furnished in the past the chief means of bridging the gap between selfish human nature and the obligations imposed by social responsibility. That the service learned by the individual in the family group has so often stopped with the family group is no condemnation of the institution of the family. It is rather merely an indication that this group, like even the nation itself, may become a stumbling block to the wider service of humanity, if it is not brought within the sweep of humanitarian ideals. But surely the ethics of service will not work in society at large unless we can get it to work first in the intimate group of the family where altruism is so strongly backed by natural affection. Because the family is the institution which has cradled the civilization of the past, we must not forget its central place in the civilization of the future. The ideal of a stable, wholesome, and sane family life must be held up before each generation if we are to conserve our most precious social possessions; and the social order must be such as to make possible for each normal individual such a family life.

Because the family has often failed to perform its high functions in the social life, is no reason for a negative attitude toward this institution. If we should condemn the family as an institution for such a reason, we should have to condemn on the same ground all human institutions. Rather our attitude should be, if we are scientific, the constructive one of searching out and correcting the faults in individual character and in social organization which have made possible the failure of the family in individual instances. It is plain that higher ideals must dominate our family life, as we showed when discussing eugenics, if it is to meet the needs of the civilization of the future. Not only must the ideal of the service of humanity dominate marriage and the family, but society in general must value the service of humanity through marriage and the family. We must conserve the human values in these institutions. We must especially recognize true motherhood and true fatherhood as among the highest forms of social service; and to this end we must educate every normal individual for the duties of marriage and parenthood. Then through the family, as the cradle of individual character, we may rationally hope to regenerate the social life in general.

Again, we must have a revaluation of government and law, if we are to solve the social problem. We have already, to be sure, a childish, almost an absurd, faith in the power of governmental machinery, and in the power of the ballot to work all sorts of social wonders. We need on the one hand, to see the limitations of what government and law can do in society; and on the other hand, we need renewed faith in government and law as regulative and integrating organs of society. The New World especially has lost in part its tradition of the place and function of government. The reproach of lawlessness has especially rested on the American people and with just reason. But this to some extent is due to the fact that

we have lost the ideals of government which
our forefathers once possessed. They believed
in a politics of patriotism, while we have had
too long dominant among us a politics of
self-interest. Not only have whole parties
been devoted to class-interests, but politicians
and even ordinary voters have often shame-
lessly confessed to being dominated by no
higher motive than their own pocketbook. It
is no wonder that under such circumstances,
with our politics and government simply an
expression of contending selfish interests, we
have lost our faith in our legislators, execu-
tives, and judiciary. The respect for law itself is lost under such conditions, because we
no longer believe in the patriotism of either
our legislators or our judges. It is evident
that democracy will not work under such circumstances, where it is nothing but a mere contention between individual and class egoisms.

We must have a renaissance of the politics
of patriotism, if democratic law and government are to endure, because no one can respect
law or government which he thinks is simply

the triumph of the selfishness of one class over the selfishness of another. A politics which is founded upon genuine love of country will, moreover, in the last analysis not be found to be antagonistic to a true humanitarianism. The service of a national group is, no more than the service of a family group, opposed to the service of humanity at large. While we must insist that, "Above all nations is humanity," yet humanity must realize itself in the smaller concrete groups from the family and the neighbourhood to the nation, which, through the development of their own solidarity, make possible that wider solidarity of humanity as a whole. Here again we must remember the important socio-psychologic principle that development of loyalty to one group, when we have an hierarchy of groups, does not weaken, but may rather strengthen the loyalty to the great group which includes all as parts.

The negative attitude toward government which grew up in Western civilization during the nineteenth century, ranging from *laissez-*

faire individualism to a doctrine of absolute anarchism, is not justified when we consider the growing complexity of social life and its increasing need of regulation. On the contrary, government will be more and more needed as civilization advances. It must cover in time practically all human interests, in such a way, however, as not to destroy individual initiative or to block normal social change. Nor must it be developed in individual nations in such a way as to prevent the federation of all governments to secure world-peace and world-order. Government within the nation must be made to serve the larger life of humanity. Yet this is practicable only when we have in the leading Western nations a free, enlightened democracy, in which the individual voter is effectively controlled by the ideal of the service of man, rather than by mere selfish, class, or national interests.

Finally, we need a rebirth of faith in democracy, in the sense of "free society"— society which "founds the common good upon the common will, in forming which it bids every grown-up, intelligent person to take a part." Such society is the only remedy for those class divisions, distrusts, and misunderstandings which threaten to tear our civilization asunder and defeat its aspirations. For there is nothing which unites and reconciles men more than that interpenetration of minds, that free exchange of ideas and ideals, that mutual understanding, which is necessary for the formation of a common or group will.

Democracy is not the *laissez-faire* individualism which in America previous to the War was too often taken for it—the doctrine that everybody should be allowed to do as he pleased, provided that he did not interfere with the "natural rights" of other individuals. Neither is it "egalitarianism," which would ignore the differences between individuals, discount the need of experts in conducting public business, and consider one man as good as another even when it comes to very responsible positions. Nor is it finally "majority rule," for in a true democracy the rights of minorities are respected and there is no autocratic rule even on the part of the majority.

Rather the foundation of democracy is fraternity. Its prototype and model is the sympathetic, understanding, like-minded family or neighbourhood group which has but one will. Like Christianity, democracy is in complex modern nations, perhaps, a counsel of social perfection. But like Christianity, it too is the hope of the world. The peoples of the world are discontented with the old authoritarian forms of government and social life, and they are groping toward a new, higher, and freer form of society. Democracy to them is what self-determination is to the individual. It reconciles men to one another, not only because it recognizes the worth of each man, counts each as one, but because it enlarges their interests and expands their lives and wills. We need more democracy as a solvent for the social problem.

Again, we must have a revaluation of religion if the social problem is to be solved. Religion especially stands for the spiritual life in man. It is essentially a projection and a universalization of social values.[68] While, like government and other agencies of social control, it may make the mistake of sanctioning the wrong values, yet because the individual needs, especially in the more complex stages of social development, to have the social values impressed upon his consciousness in the intensest way, they need to come to him essentially in a religious form. Only thus can they receive that character of universal and absolute validity which is necessary for their effective control of social action. Thus religion has in all ages proved a most powerful force working for social order. It is, as Professor Ward says, "the power of social gravitation which holds the social world in its orbit."[69] Because it is the vehicle of

[68] See the writer's article on "The Social Function of Religion" in the *American Journal of Sociology*, November, 1913; also, Ames, *The Psychology of Religious Experience*.

[69] See his article on "The Essential Nature of Religion" in the *International Journal of Ethics*, Vol. VIII, pp. 169–92.

social ideals, it is equally capable, if the ideals which it sanctions are high enough, of becoming the most powerful engine of social progress. In short, religion is peculiarly connected with the higher life of civilization, so much so, that the death of religion would probably mean the destruction of all higher social values, and therefore ultimately of the higher forms of civilization.

Now, the modern world is rapidly becoming extremely indifferent, if not agnostic, as to the claims of religion. It is listening with a more attentive ear than ever to those leaders in thought who claim that society can get along very well without religion. Religion, in other words, is very far from receiving the place which it should receive in our civilization. It is shoved off into one corner and made, like philosophy, a badge of respectability, or else it is regarded as superstition altogether.

But if our analysis of the social situation is correct, religion is needed to stimulate altruism in the mass of men. A social religion, in other words, is the one thing which can do most to save human nature from selfishness and brutality, and so to solve the social problem. By a social religion, we mean, of course, one which will exalt the service of humanity over and above the service of any individual, class, nation, or even race, as the highest end and value. Only such a religion can adequately support a humanitarian ethics, and only such, therefore, can overcome the antagonism of interest which may easily exist between races, nations, and classes. If that war between individuals, classes, nations, and races, which constitutes the heart of the social problem, is to be done away with, it must be by a religion of love and service.

Finally, we must have a revaluation of morality and of moral ideals themselves, if we are going to solve the social problem. Indeed, the family, government, and religion are all valuable only as they support moral practices or moral ideals. Yet the modern world has become strangely indifferent as regards matters of conduct. As Professor Giddings says, "We have been extremely anxious to bridge the gulf between the ignorant and the educated, and we are beginning to wake up to the importance of bridging the gulf between the rich and the poor, but we still are scarcely concerned with bridging the gulf between the vicious and the good." Yet it is just this gulf which must be bridged if the social problem is to be solved.

The virtues are what bind men together in harmonious relations; and it is idle to think that there can be a satisfactory social life without the common virtues of honesty, veracity, loyalty, and justice, to say nothing of the more transcendent qualities of the love and service of humanity as a whole. We must, therefore, wake up to the importance of moral practices and moral ideas in every sphere of our social life. We must conserve our moral ideals as our most precious spiritual possessions and make moral training the centre of our educational system. For the ultimate problem in human society is to bridge this gulf between the vicious and the just, as Professor Giddings has said. Viciousness and immorality are the anterooms to crime, and crime is the dissolution of the social order itself. We know, of course, that crime may come from defective minds, or that it may be bred by economic injustice; but far more serious to society than these two former sorts of crime, serious as they are, is the crime which is bred by the lowering of the ideals of our social life. This is the crime which may spread some day like wildfire throughout Western civilization and mark its final dissolution in moral anarchy. Civilization must depend in the last analysis upon the individual characters of the men and women who make it up.

How, then, is the gulf between the vicious and the good to be bridged in society? The reply is that men are saved, society is saved, by effective beliefs, provided of course that these beliefs are broad enough to deal properly with all factors in the situation. The question of questions for social ethics, therefore, is what system of moral ideals is best suited to promote the increasing harmony and progressive development of humanity. Now the ethics of individualism, which makes the criterion by which we shall test our moral ideals either the happiness or the self-development of individuals, has failed in Western civilization to produce either increasing social harmony or the progressive development of all humanity. Hedonistic and "self-culture" ethics, in other words, have failed to "bridge the gulf between the vicious and the good," and have even tended strongly to produce in practice in modern civilization egoistic and anti-social conduct. They are both failures from a social point of view. This has usually been seen by careful ethical thinkers, so far as "hedonistic ethics" is concerned. It has not so generally been seen as regards the "ethics of self-development," which in the nineteenth century was almost universally regarded as favourable to human progress. To a certain extent it undoubtedly is so; but, at least as popularly interpreted, it also has tended to anti-social conduct.

The ethics of individualism has, we repeat, broken down in Western civilization. Instead of helping to solve the social problem, it has tended to intensify it. What system of morality, then, will meet the needs of our complex civilization? It would seem that only a system which would put *first* the development of humanity as a whole, rather than the development, or happiness, of the individual, would be adequate for the solution of the social problem.[70] In other words, *the moral ideal must be pictured, not as a perfect man, but as a perfect society consisting of all humanity.* Practically this means for the

[70] The writer's paper referred to at the beginning of Chapter I concluded with these words: "If Western civilization is not to go down through a series of hopeless conflicts between nations and classes, it must have a re-birth of humanitarian ethics, that is, an ethics which shall teach the individual to find his self-development and his happiness in the service of others, and which shall forbid any individual, class, nation, or even race from regarding itself as an end in itself apart from the

individual that his moral ideal shall be that his life is for the service of humanity; that his self-development and even his happiness are but means to that service. The ideal of the service of humanity, however, demands the fullest development of the powers of the individual for that service and even his happiness in such service. Thus the humanitarian ideal is synthetic of all that is worth while in the hedonistic and self-culture ideals. But in the practical moral life of men it makes all the difference in the world which is emphasized—self or humanity.

Moreover, a system of morality based on the ideal of the service of humanity has the immense advantage of having the best religious traditions in Western civilization behind it; for it can scarcely be doubted by any sane

rest of humanity. The general acceptance of such an ethics would have prevented the present war; and whatever the issue of the present struggle, only the frank acceptance of such humanitarianism by the leaders of future civilization can save the world from a series of endless conflicts between classes, nations and races."

mind that such an ethics is implicit in the ethics of love and service taught by Christianity at its purest. Now, moral ideals become effective beliefs in society in proportion as they appear to have absolute validity, and this implies, we have seen, a religious sanction. The divorce of morality from religion is fatal to the social utility of either. Moral and social ideals need a socialized religion, a humanitarian ethics a religion of humanity, which will make the service of man the highest religious act.

Now, it is greatly to be regretted that not all at the present time who see the need of a humanitarian ethics see equally the need of a religion of the service of man; and, moreover, that Christianity at its purest is such a religion. Comte might be excused from failing to see in Christianity the religion of humanity which he believed necessary for the solution of the social question, because the only Christianity which he knew was that of ecclesiastical forms, narrow and unadapted to the requirements of modern life. To a large extent this is perhaps still true of the organized Christianity of the world. Much still has to be done to secure a religion, even in Western civilization, adapted to the requirements of our social life. The Church, therefore, has largely lost its hold both of the masses and of the thinking classes. But a purer, a humanized, a socialized Christianity has been gradually rising among the leading nations of Europe and America, which does seek to meet the social needs of the hour. This new Christianity lays aside theological disputation and devotes itself to the practical application of humanitarian ethics to everyday living. Now, it is much easier to reform and revitalize an existing religion than to create a new one. It would seem, therefore, that even from a strictly scientific point of view, there is need of a revaluation of Christianity by those interested in the solution of the social problem. It deserves seriously to be tried before it is cast aside. Certainly we must have a *redemptive* religion if we are to have a fully socialized ethics—one which is equal to

"bridging the gulfs" in existing humanity.[71]

One way to bridge the gulf between the
vicious and the good in society must now be
apparent and in the writer's opinion it is the
way of the greatest practical importance; and
that is, to use the proper ethical ideals to
control the development of conduct and character in the young. In other words, the proper
moral and social values must be given the
young through some system of moral education. Too long in America we have assumed
that moral and social education may be left
to take care of itself, without any specific
provision for it in our educational curricula.
But it must now be evident to all thoughtful
minds that one reason for the existing confu-

[71] Professor J. Vernon Bartlet, of Mansfield College,
Oxford (to whom the writer is indebted for many
suggestions), has pointed out that the eminent Jewish
scholar, Mr. C. G. Montefiore, in his *Religious Teaching
of Jesus* (pp. 57f.) has cordially recognized that the
"redemptive note" of Christianity is its "new idea"
and strongest trait. *Cf.* Seeley's *Ecce Homo*, chap. XIV.

sion in regard to moral and social values in our civilization, is that we have entered upon no deliberate policy of conserving them.

Moral education is usually claimed to belong especially to the Church and the home; and there can be no doubt that these institutions are best fitted to impress moral values upon the child. The Church especially, as the organized embodiment of the religious life of the people, ought to be the public conservator and propagator of ideal social values. While its function may rightly be conceived as that of being "the spiritual power" in society, its practical task in the present age must be spiritual leadership; and that means that it must become largely an educational institution. It ought to be in the best sense "an ethical culture society," a society where the highest ethical culture is given to all who come within its influence.

Unfortunately, however, as we have seen, large masses of the people are outside of any church; and even if the Church as a whole could be reawakened to the full meaning of its great mission in society, and the often petty divisions within itself healed, yet it would still probably be some time before all in Western nations alone could be effectively brought under its influence. Therefore, the burden of imparting the minimum moral education needed must be placed upon the public school system. This we shall discuss at length in the next chapter.

At the very beginning of this book we said that radical reconstruction of the spirit of our civilization was needed. What, then, must be the moral ideas upon which Western civilization must rebuild itself if it is to survive and to become world-wide? First of all, there is the idea of Humanity and its common life, as above that of any nation, race or class. Closely related with it is the idea of human brotherhood, as embracing all men, whatever their condition. Then the idea of the service of humanity, or social service, especially on the part of the stronger nations, races, classes, and individuals, toward the weaker. Then the coördinate ideas of self-development and self-sacrifice, not as ends in themselves but for the sake of the service of humanity. Then such ideas as justice, peace, and goodwill, not simply between man and man, but between races, nations, and classes. Finally the whole list of social virtues which make possible the family, the State, and the whole harmonious living together of men in groups, which has made possible human civilization.

If such humanitarian ideals were rightly taught in our schools, if they were reënforced by a humanitarian religion preached in our churches, and by a humanitarian science and philosophy taught in our universities, if, in short, they were the "mores" of our civilization, then in one generation we should have a new earth, and so a new heaven.

CHAPTER VI

THE EDUCATIONAL ELEMENT IN THE SOCIAL PROBLEM

WE said in the last chapter that science and education must become the chief means of controlling and reorganizing the society of the future. If this is so, the reconstruction of our educational system, even in the narrow sense, is fundamental in the reconstruction of our civilization. We cannot solve our social problems without social intelligence; and the easiest way to secure social intelligence is through the education of the young in our schools along social and political lines. In a democracy, the people are the masters, and they must be taught how to solve their own problems if the great experiments of free government and free society are not to fail. *The creation of social intelligence and character in the individual is the heart of our problem.* For this reason the way out in our civilization is largely through social and political education.

Yet our schools have been strangely indifferent to the need of a specific social and political education. Good citizenship, by which is meant not merely intelligent voting, important as that is, but efficient membership in a community, efficient fatherhood and motherhood, and, in general, fitness for community and national service, has until recently been given very inadequate attention in our schools. Education has not helped to solve our social problems as it should have done. Even a majority of our college graduates—and a very large majority if we include the graduates of our technical schools—have gone forth from their institutions without any adequate ideas as to the structure and aims of a democratic society and government. The very young men and women who were supposed to be trained for social leadership in such professions as the law, journalism, teaching, and social work, often spent so much time on professional technicalities that they acquired little social knowledge of the broader sort and almost no discriminating judgment in social and political matters. It is no wonder that the Great War revealed in the United States at least not only woeful ignorance regarding social and political conditions in Europe and a direful lack of competent public leaders, but also the presence among our educated classes of slackers, profiteers, and exploiters.

The great crisis in the world's affairs through which we are passing gives a new answer to the old question "What knowledge is of the most worth?" It shows plainly that the knowledge most worth while to our human world is knowledge of human beings in their relationships—of human living together and the problems involved therein. We live in a social world more than in a world of physical objects; and social knowledge is worth more than any other sort of knowledge because our chief adjustments have to be made more to men and to institutions than to things. Human relationships make or mar the world we know. They count for more in human happiness, and in the creation and preservation of all other social values, than everything else put together.

Nor is it true that common sense and common experience can any longer successfully adjust the individual to the world of human relationships, any more than it is true that in the modern world the farmer can learn adequately through common sense and experience how he should farm. The social world has become far too complex for the individual to make intelligent social adjustments to it without a large fund of scientific social knowledge. Our civilization has become such a complex system of social relationships that no one can play his part in it well without a considerable amount of general and specific social information. The new social, political, and industrial experiments which are being tried throughout our civilization demand a high degree of social intelligence for their success. Democracy itself is such an experiment. The attempt to establish democracy without adequate social and political education for the mass of citizens is bound to result in failure. If we want democracy we must educate for democracy.

Probably one reason why more definite social and political education has not been introduced into our schools in the past has been the fear that such education might work merely to maintain an established social order or even to sanction abuses of power. That education has often been so used in the past cannot be denied. Imperial Germany, indeed, furnished a glaring illustration of education so misused. *Scientific* social and political education, however, could not have this effect. We do not want social education merely for the sake of maintaining social unity and order, important as these are, but rather to make a better human world. We want an education for a free and democratic society, not for autocratic society. Let us see how it is that scientific social and political education would work toward true social freedom and social progress.

The mind is the chief organ of adaptation in man in his social as well as in his physical life. Any education which is truly socialized must aim at the freeing of the mind, the development of its powers, and the disciplining of these to social use., The freeing of the mind, however, is not an end in itself, as extreme individualists have thought, but rather is to assure a plastic, adaptable, and progressive social life. Now the social sciences involve a searching but impersonal criticism of institutions and public policies. They alone of all studies are best calculated to emancipate the mind and to introduce true moral freedom into our social life, if liberty in teaching them is maintained. Other studies may be liberalizing and liberating for the mind but none so profoundly as the social sciences, since they depend upon and develop an impersonal or scientific attitude *toward human affairs.*

But the emancipation of the mind which they bring is not one which leads to indifference or regardlessness as to human welfare. On the contrary, the social sciences search out the causes of human misery and social maladjustments. In their criticism of institutions and policies they point out economies not realized, and laws of social harmony and efficiency. In showing the sources of social evils and the way to remove them, they naturally stimulate efforts to remove these evils. In presenting to the student the conditions of human living in the community, the nation, and the world at large, they develop in him the imagination and the sense of social values which are necessary to construct a better social world. These recruit him for the cause of social progress, not so much upon the basis of humanitarian enthusiasm, as upon the basis of a clear understanding of the facts and forces which have been shown through scientific research to enter into the making or the marring of human life. Finally, the social sciences will favor true progress for they will show the need of scientific, experimental, step-by-step methods in social change, and will discourage rash experiments, such as revolutions or legislation inadequately supported by the popular will.

Probably the deeper opposition to social and political education in our schools, however, comes not from the friends of social freedom and progress, but from those who profit from existing abuses in the social order. Napoleon abolished the Academy of Moral and Political Sciences, and his attitude is typical of the autocrats of every age and place, no matter under what names they exist. Democracy has no need to fear a social and political education which is scientific.

All that we have said, of course, implies that the old educational dogma that education can be given regardless of content, that one subject is as good as another provided it is pursued far enough, is, from the social point of view, a great mistake. A socialized education which aims at the solution of our social problems must first of all give more recognition to social studies in the curriculum.

In spite of the great value of language studies as a means of entering into the social tradition, and of the natural sciences as a means of freeing the mind and as a basis for many vocations, social studies must in a sense be considered fundamental, in any worth-while training for citizenship. By social studies we mean those that are concerned fundamentally with human relationships and conditions, such as history, civics, domestic science, public hygiene, economics, politics or government, sociology, ethics, anthropology and the more elaborated or specialized branches or applications of these. Social education, of course, means much more than instruction in such studies, but for the reasons given above *the primary demand of social education is that more time be given to social studies.* At least one-third of the time of the curriculum from the elementary grades to the end of the A. B. college course should be devoted to such studies. From the standpoint of knowledge, they represent the most important part of the individual's training for intelligent citizenship. They should not be withheld from the child, even if some of the traditional subjects in the curriculum suffer. Nor should they be taught, except possibly in some of the grades, indirectly, by merely giving to some of the older subjects in the curriculum a more social content and direction. This latter may be desirable, but if accepted as sufficient, the newer social studies will be inadequately taught. No school or college, so far as the writer knows, has, however, yet accepted the educational revolution of making social studies fundamental in its curriculum. Even as electives they are usually given very inadequate recognition, except in cases where they come in as professional studies.

But social and political education cannot stop with the giving of mere information. An education which is truly socialized will have a social aim. It will not divorce by academic abstraction judgments of value from judgments of fact. On the contrary, *it will point out and seek to inculcate social values, standards, and ideals, as soon as sufficient scientific knowledge of facts has been attained on which to base scientific social standards and ideals.* Thus as soon as we have ascertained the conditions and effects of child labour, we have the knowledge on which we can base a scientific standard regarding it. If this were not so, social education would be useless. Only a social education which inculcates values will be adequate, as we have already said, for the work of reconstructing our civilization.

Social education means, then, moral education; for it will be education into community, national, and human ideals; not into those ideals as they exist, but as they ought to be in the light of full knowledge regarding human relationships. Hair-splitting theorists have long assured us that moral education in our public schools is impossible, impracticable, or useless; and hence for the most part only half-hearted attempts have been made in this direction. The best teachers, indeed, have usually recognized moral education as an essential part of education. But the standards of moral education in our schools have been too low to be adequate for social needs. In America there has been a strange, irrational fear that ethical instruction be considered religious teaching; while in Europe moral education has hitherto been entrusted to the representatives of religious denominations, with the result that sectarian differences have been emphasized and the larger issues in morality have been obscured. The net result has been that very little of the higher social morality needed to meet the problems of our complex civilization has been taught in the schools of either Europe or America.

But we cannot evade the issue. The good citizen is the highly moral citizen, and proper ethical ideals must be taught in our schools to control the development of conduct and character in the young. How shall this be done? The pressure of public opinion forced into American schools for a generation instruction on a very important moral question—the use of alcoholic beverages. The result demonstrated not only that moral instruction upon a scientific basis in our schools is possible, but showed clearly the method, that it must come through social education. Morality cannot be taught effectively as an abstraction. It must be taught through the study of the concrete problems in which the moral situation emerges. The trouble with most of the moral instruction in our schools in the past is that it has been divorced from the facts of our social life. If, however, we will base such instruction upon scientific social knowledge we can as readily inculcate ideals regarding character and conduct, family life, business, and human relations generally as we can standards of vocational excellence. In either case we do not expect such instruction to be always effective, but it will greatly aid. Moral education of the highest sort, then, if given through the study of concrete social situations, can be readily and effectively given in our schools; and it is only through such moral education of the young that we can expect to transform successfully our "mores."

But it may be asked, "What moral values shall be inculcated? What shall be the standard of moral judgment—happiness, power, or development? What shall be the unit of our moral valuations—the self, the nation-state, or humanity at large?" These questions have already been answered in previous chapters. We may add that the Great War showed clearly enough the social inadequacy of the happiness ideal of life, and that the power ideal belonged to the barbarous past. It also showed that the unit of our moral thinking cannot be the self, or the national group, but must be humanity at large. But it left us the service ideal of life, and the development ideal as our practical guides. The service ideal and the development ideal, however, are really two sides of the same ideal—the development of humanity. Service is the social side of this ideal, and must be more emphasized if our education is to become more socialized. A truly socialized education will demand that the student put into practice what he learns from the study of social conditions.

The watch-words of the school, therefore, should be self-development and social service; but the development of the individual, it should be emphasized, is for the sake of service, first the service of the family and the community, then the service of the state and nation, and finally the service of humanity at large. This will secure not only the development of the individual, but of the community, of the nation, and finally of humanity. Thus will education place itself fully in the service of social progress.

Nor can the moral education which inculcates the service ideal of life be fairly called "dogmatic." The service ideal is elastic, dynamic, experimental, and does not stifle individual conscience and judgment, though it does give a definitely social direction to the moral life. Blended with the development ideal, it will replace the old negative, repressive morality with a positive and constructive social ethics in harmony with modern scientific knowledge. For these reasons not only will it tend to harmonize the relations of individuals through the development of cooperative attitudes, but it will be highly favorable to progress. Finally, it will lead directly to that consecration of life to the service of humanity which is the essence of humanitarian religion, and without which, as we have seen, humanitarian civilization cannot hope to endure. *The inculcation of the service ideal of life—of service beginning in the smaller, primary groups but extending to all humanity—accordingly must be considered the heart and core of socialized education.*

Social education, finally, will make adequate provision for the practical and vocational element in education. To be a good citizen or to serve humanity at large, the individual must be usually self-supporting, must find his work in the world, and be able to do it well. The service ideal of life demands that everybody in normal health be occupied at some useful work. Moreover, we are beginning to perceive also that all service, all constructive effort, is of social value and perhaps more nearly of equal social worth than we had supposed. Social education would be a failure if it did not lead to the individual's finding his life work, his proper vocation in society, and furnish training for any socially useful vocation. In a democracy there is no room for a class of idlers; and for this very reason in a democracy all citizens have the right to find in the schools special aids for preparation for their life work.

But enthusiasts in vocational education have at times made serious mistakes from a social point of view. They have sometimes made the mistake of considering one's vocational activities—the activities by which one gains a livelihood—as more important than one's non-vocational activities. But in a democracy, the non-vocational activities of the citizen, as voter, neighbor, friend, parent, maker of public opinion, member of the community and of many non-vocational groups, are at least of equal importance with one's vocational activities. Again, they have sometimes made the mistake of confusing vocational education with social education in general. But vocationalization is only a part of the process of socialization. To mistake the part for the whole is a serious social mistake. In a democracy all men are citizens first before they are members of any calling, trade or profession—a fact which syndicalists and capitalists sometimes alike overlook. *Hence preceding all vocational education should come the liberation of the mind, the understanding of social facts, and the appreciation of social values.* An efficient lawyer, or farmer, or engineer is not necessarily a good citizen. The common experience of life shows this plainly enough. Vocational education obviously can be freed from social danger only by attaching it to a general programme of social education. The larger part of our grade work, our high school work, and our undergraduate work in college must be kept free from vocational training in order that the more general training for citizenship which we have indicated may be rightly given. Vocational education, however, should be the crown of a socialized system of education, and ample opportunities for vocational training should be open even to the child of the humblest citizen.

If even one whole generation could receive the civilian training we have outlined—mental, social, moral, vocational—our social problems would soon be in a process of solution. But there are many practical difficulties to the immediate realization of such a programme. The coöperation of the teacher, the nation, and the university will first have to be obtained. Only teachers with social vision could give such training. The teaching profession must be taught to look upon itself as a social service profession, and the individual teacher must regard himself as a social creator. He should see that his work is nothing less than to mould the social future. But to do this successfully and to understand his social function, the teacher himself must be socially educated. Economic, political, and sociological knowledge would give him vision of his social mission, and are more essential to his success than psychological knowledge of pedagogical methods. Particularly does the teacher need sociology to do his work rightly—for light upon the educational problem of the present and upon the general social significance and meaning of education. We must have sociologically trained teachers and educational administrators before we can have a successful system of social education.

The nation should be the unit for social and political education, and in the United States the agency of the federal government must be invoked for its final establishment. Good citizenship is a national concern; indeed, there is no other national concern which approaches it in importance. Training for good citizenship cannot be safely left wholly to local authorities. The unity and progress of the nation demand a national system of education. The War revealed in a striking way the need in the United States of education organized on a national scale. With from ten to thirty-five per cent of American young men between the ages of twenty-one and thirty-one in the various military camps found practically illiterate by the military authorities, with less than one-half of American children who attend school ever completing the "grades," it seems idle to discuss universal social education. It is evident that, in order that social education or civilian training may become general, practically the entire population must receive not only elementary but also secondary education.

These facts, however, emphasize that education is a national concern, the vital national concern; and that social reconstruction worth while is impossible without reconstruction in our education. We must have a reconstruction of our education which will aim to develop national and social idealism and fit the nation as a whole for the realization of its high destiny. To accomplish this, education must have national support and be organized on a national scale. This has been recognized in reconstruction plans in Great Britain, but not fully as yet in the United States.

Nor is there any danger that through a national system of education we would be led to imitate Imperial Germany and introduce a system of fostering national egoism. In a democracy there is nothing to fear from a national system of education and much to hope; and for the reasons already pointed out social and political education in a democracy would be the most effectual means of checking the very tendencies which we condemned in the autocratic German state. Even less ground is there for fearing that a national system of education might interfere with private and local initiative in education. Just as state systems of education in our various American states have left free every local community to surpass, if it chooses, the minimum standard of education set by the state, so a national system would leave free any state to *surpass* the minimum national standard. Again, our state systems of education have found it convenient to leave the field of education open to private initiative, provided that private schools conform to certain standards; so, too, would a national system. A national system of education only means that the nation will set the minimum standard of education for every community within its borders and enter into genuine coöperation with local authorities in solving the educational problem.

The university must be the vital agency in the initiation and establishment of social education, since it trains, for the most part, the social and educational leaders who shape the opinion and policy of the country. If the colleges and universities are lacking in the spirit of social service, if they do not stand for training for citizenship, if they do not encourage social research, and if they do not aid in the diffusion of scientific social knowledge, it is idle to dream of socializing education. Some universities have been attempting to work toward this ideal, but most of them in the past have been asleep to their social opportunities and responsibilities. The university, indeed, is the natural leader, the natural unit for the scientific reconstruction of our social life.[72] The university must lead, as it has been given the place of leadership in our educational system.

Besides its provisions for adequate instruction in social studies for its undergraduates and the inculcation of the spirit of social service in connection with all of its courses, it is especially its provisions for the training of social leaders along all lines which makes the university the vital agency in social reconstruction, and so in solving the social problem. Without leadership human societies would show no more capacity for progress than animal groups; but with trained,

[72] Read White and Heath, *A New Basis for Social Progress.*

expert leadership, on the other hand, their capacity for progress might be increased many fold. The solution of the social problem, therefore, practically depends upon the finding and training of social leaders.

Now, Professor Lester F. Ward demonstrated in his *Applied Sociology* that there is probably no lack of individuals in present society with natural endowments for leadership. It is simply a question of finding and training this material in our population. Particularly upon our universities would seem to rest the responsibility of finding and training social leaders. Very few of them, however, have as yet taken this responsibility seriously. The universities have long since recognized their responsibility for producing experts in the older vocations and professions—in law, in medicine, in agriculture, and in engineering; but as yet only very inadequately their responsibility for producing experts in dealing with the problems of human living together. Yet these latter experts are the ones most needed at the present time if Western civilization is to enter upon a new era of peace, harmony, and prosperity. Will the universities of the world awake to their responsibilities of providing this social leadership?

CHAPTER VII

THE SOLUTION OF THE SOCIAL PROBLEM

THE solution of the social problem requires neither superhuman intelligence nor superhuman character. Neither god-like minds nor angelic dispositions are necessary for right human living together. A satisfactory adjustment of the relations of individuals, classes, nations, and even races is by no means beyond the powers of humanity. This does not mean, however, on the one hand, that much accumulation of knowledge, both of human nature and of human society, is not still necessary before this greatest task of civilization can be achieved; nor does it mean that the present character of the mass of individuals will not have to be radically modified before a satisfactory solution of the human problem can be reached.

There is, of course, no permanent solution of the social problem possible. In a world of change, each age is necessarily confronted by new problems which it alone can solve. Our quest must not be for a static solution, but for principles which may guide us in seeking some rational control over the relations of men to one another. Now, as we have already seen in the preceding chapters, such principles, even in the present state of the social sciences, are by no means wanting. If we applied even our present available knowledge, we could soon have a very much better human world. The truth is that we have not yet become seriously interested in the social problem. We have been so interested in the conquest of nature and in individual achievement, that the problems of human relationships have not greatly concerned us; our civilization, as we have previously insisted, has had hitherto a strong materialistic and individualistic bias. We have seen that in our educational system no adequate recognition has yet been given to social studies in the curriculum, but much attention to the physical sciences and to self-culture studies.

If we would take as seriously the solution of the social problem as the conquest of nature, wonders might be accomplished even in a single generation.

No external machinery of social organization can possibly solve the problem. The desire to solve it in this way is popular to-day because it seems the easiest way and because it spares us raising bothersome questions concerning individual intelligence and character. But we have seen that society is at bottom the inter-mental life of individuals; that it is the overlapping of selves; and that while external forms of organization are important, they do not go to the root of the matter. This is the common mistake made by many socialists, pacifists, feminists and others. That external social machinery will save, is one of the sweetest delusions cherished by man in all ages in every department of social life—in religion, in morals, in government, in education, even in international relationships.

The social life of man, of course, can express itself only through organization. But it is idle to think that organization can work without the development of appropriate habits, opinions, and standards in the mass of individuals. A social institution is much more than social machinery. It is a *sanctioned* way of living. It is the spirit, as Montesquieu saw, which makes laws effective. A League of Nations, for example, to guarantee the peace of the world and promote the general welfare of mankind, cannot succeed unless there is the proper spirit back of it. It must be backed up, in other words, by an international consciousness as to the desirability of peace and of international coöperation, by the general perception and acceptance of the fact of the solidarity of mankind. Such a world organization in some form has become indispensable. Civilization, once local, is now world-wide. Contacts have multiplied between nations without a corresponding development of the machinery of control. Hence international anarchy has resulted. We have an interdependent world, and to be safe we must have some form of world organization. Yet nothing is clearer than that as long as the nations continue to think dominantly in terms of national self-interest such an organization will have insuperable difficulties.

There is, then, nothing that can prevent wars in Western civilization between nations and classes except the dominance in the mass of individuals, or at least in their leaders, of intelligence and of the ideals of peace and human solidarity—nothing, in other words, except a change in our "mores." We need right social organization to perfect and make efficient our social life, but *no social machinery can, independent of character and intelligence in individuals, save society from catastrophes*, to say nothing of solving the social problem.

Nor can the social problem be solved by paying attention to but one aspect of man's social life, to but one line of facts. All that

we have written has been an argument to
show the dangerousness and inadequacy of
one-sided views and one-sided movements in
society. The eugenists, for example, see the
central place of individual character in the
social life, but many of them pay attention to
only one line of facts connected with character, namely, the facts of heredity. The economic thinkers and historians see the importance of economic facts, but many of them forget the equal importance of religion and moral
ideals. Religious teachers see the vital importance for higher civilization of right religious and ethical ideas and ideals, but in the
past they have generally overlooked the great
influence of the industrial system and the
general social order upon the lives of men.
Political scientists emphasize the importance
of governmental and social organization, and
often quite forget the other factors which
mould individual character.[73]

Now, we must get rid of these one-sided

[73] Compare Chapter XVIII in the writer's *Sociology
in Its Psychological Aspects.*

ideas and ideals if we are to have true progress in our social life; for they all breed dangerous negative attitudes toward other elements of value in our civilization. We must replace them by a synthetic view of our social life. We must see that human nature and human society are functions of many variables; and that for any effective control over either attention must be paid to all factors of importance. We shall not succeed in straightening out our social life by straightening out simply our economic system, or our government, or our religion, or our sanitary conditions; nor shall we succeed by paying attention merely to one of these at a time; for the social life is a unity. For a well-balanced social progress, therefore, we need a synthesis of social movements as well as of social theories. But we need the synthetic view first as an instrument for well-rounded social development. A social philosophy of some sort must guide any highly conscious social movement. If social work and social legislation are not to be mere dabbling with superficial aspects of the social problem, they must be based upon a scientific study of the whole of our social life.

Finally, the social problem cannot be solved by any sudden or revolutionary change. This is, indeed, but a corollary easily deduced from the inadequacy of external or partial changes in the social life. If by "revolution" we mean simply sudden social change of any sort, then both history and psychology show that such a method rarely produces profound or lasting change for the better in the character of individuals or of nations. The socially better is built up only through raising the whole level of knowledge, of ideas, of values in a social group; and this as a rule can be done only gradually. Hence when certain sudden social transitions in history are carefully studied, they are found to have been long in preparation. It is only survivals of institutions long outgrown which can be quickly got rid of. Habits are changed in masses of men only by changing the opinions, values and habits of the individuals who make up the mass; and this generally necessitates that mental attitudes be changed in the young, through controlling in them the development of habits and ideals, that is, through education.

If, on the other hand, we mean by "revolution" the violent seizure by a non-ruling class of the power held by a ruling class, then history shows the inadequacy of this method to solve the social problem. Even in a political sense it is a desirable method of change only when the ruling class is hopelessly out of adjustment with its group, when its power is a mere survival, blocking the path of progress. But as a general method of social reconstruction or reformation, it is hopelessly inadequate, not only because it is relatively external, but chiefly because it stimulates so frightfully the forces which make for social disorder. The violent seizure of power by one class to accomplish its ends can rarely take place without bloody conflicts with other classes. As we have already pointed out, the primitive animal instincts of man, which civilization controls with such difficulty, are thus released. The question how far violence can be successfully employed in the higher stages of civilization, without defeating the ends for which it is employed, becomes, therefore, the question at issue in the doctrine of "social evolution through revolution."

So far as social science can throw light upon this question, it would seem that there are distinct limits upon the use of force in human society, and that in the higher stages of civilization the use of violence is a process of re-barbarization. It is absolutely destructive of the higher social values which the civilizing process has so painfully built up, and by which men have slowly learned to regulate their conduct. It is a reversion, in fine, to the rule of mere force, which is the essence of barbarism. If long persisted in, it must result in the total destruction of anything worthy to be called civilization. The use of violence, then, in the higher forms of human association, must defeat the very ends for which it might seemingly be rationally employed. And if this is true in the family of nations, it applies with ten-fold force to the relations of individuals and classes within the nation. All that can be said in condemnation of war in general, can be said with even greater emphasis against civil wars.

"But," it may be said, "you have yourself shown that the method of social change by revolution is inevitable if more normal methods of change fail. Why do you, therefore, condemn it?" [74]

The reply is that revolution is not a *normal* method of social change; that it marks the breakdown of the normal means of social development; that it is not inevitable, but may easily be avoided by plasticity in social institutions and in the mental attitudes of classes and individuals; and finally, that it is the business of social science to show "a more excellent way," since this pathological method of social change is so apt to be destructive of all the higher achievements of civilization. Particularly is revolution inexcusable in modern democratic societies. There government

[74] *Sociology in Its Psychological Aspects*, pp. 163–72.

is supposed to be the will of all the people and the governing class the servants of the people. If the governing class will keep in touch with the needs of all classes; if those in authority in law, in industry, in education, in religion will seek first the public good; if all classes will seek to keep open the means of understanding and sympathy with all other classes, there will be no more need of revolution as a means of social progress than there is of children's diseases in individual development. We would emphasize. however, that the responsibility for avoiding revolution rests especially upon the socially dominant classes. If they will keep free public criticism and discussion, thought and speech, and all the means of forming rational public opinion and of selecting authorities to carry out the same, there will be little or no danger of revolution being resorted to in any social group.

So our hope of solving the social problem must be not through revolution, external machinery, or one-sided reforms, but through the education of the young, the transformation of the "subjective environment" of ideals and values in society, and the development of a well-balanced programme of social progress. The development of a fuller social intelligence and social character in the individual is the heart of our problem. Practically it becomes, therefore, largely the problem of social leadership and social education. Social machinery and even social "mutations" may assist, but they are powerless without the inner, spiritual transformation of our social life, since that life consists in the mental attitudes which individuals maintain toward one another.

Now, this confession that individual character—including in that phrase the whole active nature of the individual, his impulses, his habits, his intelligence, his values and ideals— lies at the root of the social problem is scouted by many of the social thinkers of our age; for they suppose that such a confession is equivalent to a confession that the social problem, in any or all of its aspects, is insoluble. They say, "How can the development of individual character be controlled in so many millions? We might as well give up the task before we attempt it."

The reply is that science has now shown us the roots of character in the individual, that it is largely a social product and may be controlled in its development. Scientific analysis shows that there are three chief roots of individual character of which we have need to take account in our efforts to solve the social problem. These roots are heredity, the general social environment, and personal education. In one way or another we have already considered all of these in their bearing upon the social problem of the present; but let us again briefly review them.

The child must have a right start in life, a normal physical heredity, if he is to develop a normal character and function properly in his relations as an individual with other individuals. His environment may be in every respect favourable, his opportunities for personal education all that can be desired, and yet if he is born with a defective brain, he will probably fall into the socially depressed classes, or at least behave abnormally in his social relationships. Heredity is one root of individual character, and for this reason there is need of a rational eugenics programme in society, as we have seen.

The mass of individuals are, however, born relatively normal, and their character is largely determined by the pressure of the general social environment and by their personal education. There is no doubt that institutions determine individual character within certain limits. This we can readily see if we will observe the effect of the economic system under which we live upon ourselves. Our character is largely influenced by our occupations, and for the mass of individuals occupation is as frequently a matter of necessity as of free choice. An individual of normal natural endowments and perhaps above the average in education in our present society may easily find himself in an economic situation in which he becomes without work, dependent, and finally practically forced into vice and crime. A just economic order in which people can live and work is evidently an indispensable condition for the normal development of individual character. Bad social machinery or organization, in other words, can easily hamper the development or expression of good character.

Another illustration of the effect of the social environment upon individual character is seen in the pressure of social standards, ideals, and values. This "subjective environment" of the individual, consisting largely of what is known as "social tradition," plays such a large part in the formation of character that many would make it outweigh all other factors. A "social atmosphere" in which there are the proper "mores" or standards is, at least, as necessary for the normal moral development of the individual as is a physical atmosphere of a certain chemical composition for his physical development. If it does not determine the proper development of individual character, it is, at any rate, an indispensable condition for it. It is, moreover, an active agent in furthering development in certain directions. No one can live in an atmosphere of hate, egoism, or vice without absorbing some of those qualities; and the opposite is equally true. We need, therefore, an atmosphere of love, of goodwill, of mutual service between individuals, classes, and nations if we are going to solve the social problem.

The power of the "subjective environment," or "social atmosphere," is especially seen in the influence of the socially negative doctrines which prevail in Western civilization. It is doubtful if the Great World War ever would have taken place, if the predatory tradition, the doctrine of the spoliation of one's competitors as the surest means of advancing one's self, had not such a hold on Western nations. Again, it is well known that egoistic, *laissez faire*, and contract theories of society have had a profound influence upon legislation and even upon intimate personal relations, such as the family life. On the other hand, a social atmosphere surcharged with such social theories and doctrines as those of social obligation, social responsibility and social service might make all the difference in the world in individual character and in social life. We should see by this time, at any rate, the futility of holding up self-interest as a guide in the social life, and then hoping to solve the social problem by striking a balance between egoisms, whether of individuals or groups.

We must conclude, then, that the general social environment or organization has a great influence upon the development and expression of individual character, and that this is particularly true of the industrial system and of socially prevalent doctrines, standards, and values—in brief, the "mores."

It is difficult, though convenient, to distinguish the effects of personal education from the effects of the latter. But the former is brought about by the still narrower, artificial environment of the home and the school. Its influence, moreover, upon the formation of habit, opinions, and ideals—of the whole character—of the young, growing individual is so tremendous that it demands separate consideration. For it is probably the easiest way of attempting the control of heredity and of the social environment. The general social organization may be on a high level and a man's heredity normal, but if his personal education has been neglected or vicious, he will probably be a dangerous member of society. On the other hand, though the social life may be far from what it ought to be, if a man can be given through personal education the proper ideas and ideals he may prove a savior of his group.

Now let us illustrate how this control of heredity, of social environment, and of education will work toward the solution of the social problem. Let us take one simple, but profound aspect of that problem—namely, crime. Scientific research has shown beyond

question that a part of the criminal class are
hereditary defectives, and that their criminal-
ity is due predominantly to this fact. Another
part of the criminal class seem to be normal
individuals, but are victims of their social
environment: the industrial system or the
vicious standards of their groups, as e. g.,
the drink habit, have played the main part
in their downfall. Finally, in a part of the
criminal class neglected or vicious education in
the home and the school seem to be responsible for their condition. Now, if industrial
organization were perfectly just and the social
atmosphere all that it should be, we should
still be very far from eliminating crime, if
we did not control the factor of hereditary defectiveness; and so, conditions being changed,
with the other factors. If on the other
hand, we could properly control heredity,
the social environment, and personal education
we could eliminate all crime in society, except the small amount due to accident. The
problem of crime is, then, not insoluble, and
the methods by which its solution must be

sought illustrate the ways in general by which the solution of the social problem should be sought.

Let us now take a more complex aspect of the social question—the labour problem. An externally perfect economic organization of society would not solve this problem, for if there were still individuals lacking good judgment and character, there would still be exploitation of the weak by the strong. As an able financial writer has recently shown,[75] any improvement in the economic status of the labouring class without a corresponding increase in their intelligence and character would result in no permanent advantage to them. Sooner or later the very fact that they were on a lower level of potential social efficiency than other classes would count against them, and they would tend to become socially depressed. He argues that the deepest interest, therefore, of the labouring class, as well as of all classes in society, is in

[75] Babson, *The Future of the Working Classes*, First Section.

increasing the social power and efficiency of its individual members; and that this is largely a matter of proper education. If the labouring class would aim at the domination in their interest of the school system, rather than at the domination of the legal and industrial systems, they would more certainly insure the improvement of their social status and their domination of society as a whole.

Now, the labour problem illustrates the complexity of the general social problem. It is usually assumed, on the one side of the controversy, that all that is needed for its solution is a juster industrial order; on the other side, that moral ideals in employers and employees would suffice to solve the question. But when the problem is studied carefully its solution is seen to involve, as we have seen, not only changes in the educational system, but radical changes in the whole social and industrial order, in social standards and values, and some control of hereditary defects. In other words, we cannot control the development of individual character without control of the social environment in which the individual lives as well as of the educational system. The solution of the labour problem requires, therefore, like that of the social problem in general, the proper control of the three roots of character, heredity, social environment, and personal education, of all classes, both employers and employees; nor is this beyond the scope of a practicable programme.

But if the control of individual character is the crux of the social problem, granting that that is possible, what sort of character shall we aim at? The reply is that sociology and psychology have demonstrated that for the proper social adjustment of the individual at least two things are necessary in his character: First, the predominance of intelligence over mere impulse or instinct; secondly, the predominance of the altruistic impulses over the egoistic impulses. In other words, reason must be made to prevail over blind impulse and emotion; and altruism, regard for others, over the selfish tendencies of human nature. Now, human nature, as given to us, is particularly weak in both of these points: it is naturally impulsive and is apt to be irrational; and its other-regarding impulses are weaker than its self-regarding. The whole system of society, and especially of personal education, must be such as to stimulate the development of the rational and altruistic sides of human nature, and duly to repress mere instinct and mere egoism, if we are to develop a sufficiently strong social character in the individual.

This does not mean that the self-regarding impulses and sentiments of the individual should be suppressed, as some have assumed, a thing which would be both impossible and undesirable. It only means that the strong, self-regarding impulses should be harnessed, as it were, and controlled by the altruistic impulses. Only thus can we get strong individuality. Again, it does not mean that altruism, or humanitarian sentiment, is by itself a sufficient guide in social life. On the contrary, unintelligent altruism is as great a danger in society as abstract, dehumanized intelligence. Intelligence and altruism must work together to produce the fully socialized character. Practically, it may be remarked, the principle of the dominance of reason and altruism in individual character means in social terms the dominance of science and of humanitarian ethics and religion in society. Humanitarian religion and ethics would be blind without science, but science without such a religion and ethics would lack motive power.

Now, Comte thought that if reason and altruism could be made to prevail in individual character and in social life, that would be the solution of the social problem. The modern spirit would perhaps insist upon a third thing as equally necessary, and that is, efficiency. It may perhaps be justly urged that efficiency is a product of intelligence and socialized character. This may be true of the all-round efficiency of the citizen; but there are certain sorts of efficiency, that of the expert in any line for instance, which could not be produced

by the mere dominance of the intellect over
the instincts and of other-regard over self-
regard. Special training in special lines would
in addition be required. Now, the function
of the expert is steadily becoming of increasing importance in our social life; and therefore specialized efficiency along many lines
may play a great part in the solution of the
social problem. Still, from a general social
point of view it may reasonably be maintained that intelligence and altruistic character in the individual are more necessary
than specialized efficiency, since all must be
citizens before they are experts or members
of any trade or profession, and since over-
specialization must be avoided in order to
produce the all-round human qualities which
make the good citizen. At any rate, if the
world had taken seriously these ideas of
Comte, it might have been saved much of its
present trouble.

Perhaps Novicow, the great Russian sociologist, however, more happily phrased it
when he found the solution of the social

problem in what we may term "mutualism."
Men live together, he said, by the mutual
exchange of services, goods, and sacrifices.[76]
In proportion as there is relative equality in
render'ng each other mutual service, in that
proportion men succeed in living together
harmoniously and mutually advantageously.
If A gives all to B and receives nothing in
return, then manifestly A will soon be exhausted and perish. Or if A gives more to B
than B returns to A, the service will be un-
equal and again A must soon become exhausted and perish. If, on the other hand,
B gives as much to A as A gives to B, there
is full reciprocity of service established. The
relation is then harmonious because it is just,
and association can indefinitely continue.
Only when there is this relative equality of
service rendered can there be a stable adjustment between individuals or groups which
can indefinitely persist.

[76] See his *Mechanism and Limits of Human Association* (translation in *Am. Journal of Sociol.*, Vol. XXIII,
pp. 289–349.

Yet individuals, classes, and nations have all through human history been under the illusion that they can get good for themselves through the despoiling or exploitation of other individuals, classes, or nations; that is, getting something from these latter for which they do not give or seek to give any equivalent return. It may be admitted that B may profit for a time by despoiling A, yet as he destroys the basis of their common welfare, it cannot profit him in the long run. By despoiling A, B has exchanged a continuing benefit which might have come from reciprocity with A for a temporary profit.

Now, this very simple analysis brings us to the heart of the social problem, the problem of the relations of men and of groups of men to one another. It is evident that only as the ideal of mutual service, of reciprocity in conferring mutual benefits (or even, if need be, in mutual sacrifices), controls men in their relations can there be stable and harmonious human living together. Such are the mores of true civilization as opposed to those of barbarism, which are those of spoliation and exploitation. Yet men have everywhere failed to grasp this truth, the truth of the solidarity of their interests. All through even the so-called Christian centuries the mass of men, owing to the survival of the predatory traditions of barbarism, have continued to be under what Novicow calls the "spoliation illusion," the illusion that they can live profitably at the expense of other men, or can profit by the suffering of others. From this illusion has sprung the attempts of nations and classes to dominate or exploit one another. Largely from it also has sprung the mistaken idea that wrong should be repaid by wrong, that we can remedy an injury by doing an injury in return.

It is evident that if we are to get rid of the strife which constantly threatens between classes, nations, and races in the modern world, we must get rid of the inadequate ideas which have guided men in their relations in the past. There must be, instead, general

276

acceptance of the truth that men live together happily and successfully through goodwill and mutual service—through recognition of the solidarity of their interests. As we have seen, it is our mores—our social values and standards—which make our civilization and largely shape the character of individuals. If we want true civilization we must first get rid of the mores of barbarism which linger among us. We rid ourselves but yesterday of slavery, fixed social classes, and political autocracy. But we still have with us militarism, class exploitation, national and racial egoism, and "predatoriness" still characterizes much of our business, our politics, and even our personal relations. It is idle to talk of radical social reconstruction unless we change our mores. If we transform them from those of barbarism into those of a humanitarian, Christian civilization, we shall find reconstruction along every needed line easy. But if we do not make progress toward such a transformation of our mores, even political and economic programmes of reconstruction will fail. Thus economic justice, for example, cannot be established, as we have already insisted, upon the basis of the self-interest standards which have hitherto dominated our business world. Nor will working men and employers get together in harmonious relations to build the prosperity of the future as long as they are ruled by selfish and class interests. There must first be recognition of a solidarity of interest transcending that of class.

But how can our mores be transformed? The answer is that through all human history they have been transformed in but one way, and that is through the process of learning. Progress is essentially a process of learning better adjustments on the part of the mass of individuals. War has often transformed the mores, but only because it has taught men through its hard lessons. In times of peace, however, the mores can be most successfully transformed by the education of the masses. We do not refer merely to the work of the schools, though that as we have seen must be considered central and fundamental, but to all organized effort to spread knowledge, to mould opinion, to form standards, and to develop socially advantageous habits. This is the process by which the mores of a true civilization are built up.

But such a process of social education for the masses can obviously be successful only if we have a sufficient number of trained social leaders. We see again, therefore, that the solution of the social problem depends upon the finding and training of social leaders; and that that must be in the main the work of our schools. It has not been our purpose to outline in detail a programme of social reconstruction, though we have pointed out in our discussion of principles the measures which we believe to be most important. But in concluding our discussion of principles it is fitting that we reëmphasize that social progress does not come automatically, that it must be intermediated by thought and effort; that a process of social reconstruction, if it is to endure, must be an educational process; and that education is therefore all-important in social reconstruction. We shall build the superior society of the future just as we produce the superior engine—by scientifically trained minds that know social facts and forces so that they can map out and plan a superior social organization which in turn shall produce individuals of superior intelligence and character.

But there is a necessary preliminary—and that is a general social awakening. It is possible that the Great War has caused such a general social awakening in Western civilization, and thus it has aroused in students of social conditions large hopes. Whatever its losses, it has clarified some of our ideas and shown us the path we must take if we would avoid even greater dangers. Thus far, we must admit, mankind has learned chiefly by calamities. The crisis through which we have just passed, if we will not forget it, may prove a stimulus to call forth our noblest constructive efforts. It may mean the birth of a new civilization. Aristotle had the theory that the purpose of tragedy was to purge the human soul. So the tragedy of the Great War may purge our civilization of the influences which have lingered in it from the barbarous past and which threaten its disruption. Through making us take thought it may possibly enable us to build a new and better civilization, one based upon the recognition of the solidarity of humanity, and with service, rather than power, as its final standard.

INDEX

283

INDEX

INDEX

F

Family, the, decay of, 23, 43; Hebrew concepts based on, 55, 56; eugenics, 139; solidarity, 177, 199; revaluation, 198–200

Feeble-minded, the, see Abnormal classes

Feminism, 13, 250

Ferrero, Guglielmo, cited, 3, 30, 76, 82, 97, 136

Figgis, J. N., cited, 8, 167

Fisher, Irving, cited, 100

Force, the use of, see Revolutions and Militarism

Free society, 67, 84

Freedom, of public criticism, discussion, thought and speech, 259

Frontier, influence of, 89, 90

G

Galton, Sir Francis, cited, 113, 119, 120, 136, 142

Geographic determinism, see Determinism

German civilization, 26, 27

Giddings, F. H., cited, 88, 211, 212

Goddard, H. H., cited, 111

Government, social function of, 170–185, 202–207

Greece, Ancient, civilization, 53, 54, 57, 58; ethics, 59; artistic individualism, 59, 60; philosophy, 62, 63; corruption, 61, 66; influence through the Renaissance, 73, 78

Group egoism, 10, 44, 265

H

Habit, social, 18

Hayes, Carlton, J. H., 164

Health, public, 98–102

Hebrew ethics and religion, conquest of Western world by, 51, 52, 53; high development, 54, 55, 56; expansion into Christianity, 69, 70; conflict with Greek philosophy, 71, 72, 73; eugenic character, 142

Hedonistics ethics, 75, 213

Henderson, C. R., cited, 173

Heredity, theory, 105, 106; control, 12, 18, 40, 102, 103, 113, 117, 143, 144, 233; Weismann's law, 107, 108, 109; Mendel's law, 110, 111, 112; overemphasis of importance, 115, 225

Historical elements in social problem, 42, 48–91

History, as a method of social science, 48

Hobhouse, L. T., cited, 36, 48, 115, 172

Humanitarianism, in Hebrew ethics, 56, 57, 58; in eighteenth and nineteenth centuries, 85, 86; in eugenics movement, 104, 144; in a social religion, 210–216, 221, 271

Hygiene, public, 98–102, 174

Hyper-nationalism, German, 43, 44; Jewish, 70

I

Idealism, social, 26, 191–221

Ideological theory of history, 192

INDEX

INDEX

INDEX

/3/09